'A must-read book for any
new role and for those alr
need of directic

Maria Northwood, HR

THE

STEP-UP

MINDSET

FOR SENIOR

MANAGERS

MARGO MANNING

The Step-Up Mindset for Senior Managers

First published in 2021 by

Panoma Press Ltd
48 St Vincent Drive, St Albans, Herts, AL1 5SJ, UK
info@panomapress.com
www.panomapress.com

Book layout by Neil Coe.

Printed on acid-free paper from managed forests.

ISBN 978-1-784529-39-0

DEDICATION

Dedicated to three of the greatest female
teachers in my life:

My mum, for not seeing my limitations and
imperfections and not allowing me to use them
as excuses.

My sister Lou, for reminding me to laugh more
and that includes at myself.

And Rachael Leigh, one of my strongest
collaborators in life and business.

Hubbs and Magoo, just because.

TESTIMONIALS

An excellent handbook for new senior managers that arms them with the structure to succeed in their new role.

Tony Falltrick, Senior Leader, Service Management & Operations Consultant, Top FTSE 100 organisations

A must-read book that will lead you up those steps on to senior management!

Colin Fulcher, Project Manager (Rothesay Townscape Heritage), Argyll and Bute Council

A brilliant, easy to read and clear introduction to the senior manager role and the skills associated with it.

Vesta Leikaite, Project Manager, Zutec

If this book had existed when I was on my journey to senior management, it would have been an invaluable travel companion.

Sandra Young, Head of Modern Foreign Languages, St Gregory's Catholic Science College

It is clear from the off that the author has experience within leadership. In this book you gain a greater sense of the role and responsibilities of a senior manager, alongside the possible successes and pitfalls. The book offers practical advice that can be implemented immediately, whilst providing the toolkit to manage both effectively and efficiently. It reminds us to take a breath and reflect on our personal impact and performance and how this adds or detracts from our brand and reputation.

A must-read book for anyone looking to step up into a new role and for those already within the role who are in need of direction and development.

Maria Northwood, HR Director, Axis Europe PLC

ACKNOWLEDGEMENTS

Tony Falltrick, for the support on making this book part of a series.

Colin Fulcher, your ongoing support and book review is priceless.

Vesta Leikaite, thank you for the fantastic new friendship and book review.

Maria Northwood, it is great working with you and thank you for your review and feedback.

Kai Maltman, for the final push I needed to get me started. Looking forward to reading your book.

Brooke Maltman, the best.

Russell Measor, thank you for sharing your thoughts and ideas, they were gratefully received.

CONTENTS

Chapter 2 - Managing your working styles, responses and behaviours   57

INTRODUCTION

Welcome to *The Step-Up Mindset for Senior Managers*. This is the second book in the series of 'The Step-Up Mindset'. The first book, *The Step-Up Mindset for New Managers*, was formulated to support, provide focus and develop the reader within their managerial career. This book takes you on the next step in your managerial career. It is written for all those individuals who aspire to move to the next step, namely a senior manager's role. The book is written for existing senior managers who are new to their role or have received no formal development.

This book focuses on your personal development, centred around three vital areas of responsibility: self, business and team management. The objective of the book is to enhance and prepare both your mindset and your skill set in becoming an outstanding senior manager. Focusing on the mindset will drive the correct behaviours, rounding this off with the required skill set will allow you to become an effective, efficient and successful senior manager.

Each chapter is followed with an opportunity to reflect on the chapter details and how this resonates with you, and to carry out a series of exercises that will build your understanding. This includes reflecting on your motivations for your career aspirations, your working styles, responses and behaviours and their impact on others, and the issues with always firefighting and living in the drama. Hard fact, you, the manager, are often the catalyst of your team's troubles. Review how to and the importance of coaching your team, understanding and implementing the company's strategic plan, developing your business acumen, creating a high-performance culture, working towards continuous business improvement, implementing change and demonstrating your worth to your manager and the business.

It is a manager's role, regardless of level of seniority, to carry out the role efficiently and effectively. It is your responsibility as a senior manager to ensure that you are supporting the business's success, and closely followed by having a duty of care to your team, that duty of care includes and is not exclusive to the individuals' wellbeing, both physically and mentally. To meet your goals and that of the business, you will be required to grow and sustain a team who are motivated and productive.

There are many layers to a business, to simplify this there are four key areas that you as a senior manager must focus your attention on: business goals, client requirements, team requirements and self, and not necessarily in that order. Understanding what business success looks like, matching the client requirements to the business needs and vice versa, managing your team's requirements and your own, will create a sustainable environment. Your personal reputation and brand as a senior manager and that of your team and in turn your company will be cemented during this time.

This chapter will briefly cover some of the foundations, if you are 100% comfortable with the topic, skip ahead. However, they are brief paragraphs and you may learn something by reading it.

MANAGEMENT LEVELS

Depending upon a company's management structure, you may find that there are multiple layers of management, typically assigned to a strong hierarchical culture. On the other side, there are companies who have a flat hierarchical structure. For the purposes of this book, we are taking the simplest route, that is there are three levels of management: first-line managers, senior managers and executive leaders.

First-line managers

Most senior managers, at some point in their career and possibly directly prior to promotion to senior manager, will have served in a first-line manager's role. Typically, a first-line manager's role is to follow a brief from senior managers and ensure that day-to-day operations happen seamlessly. Ideal world thinking, of course, real world execution isn't always that plain sailing.

First-line managers are responsible for reactive management and day-to-day operational tasks.

Senior managers

The senior manager's role is to translate the company's strategic business plan into a working brief to be shared with their first-line managers. In addition to this, the senior manager will strive to improve business health through continued business improvement plans whilst supporting their team and their executive leadership team.

The senior manager is responsible for meeting the proactive, strategic requirements of the executive leadership team and the reactive, operational management of their direct reports, typically first-line managers.

Executive leaders

The executive leader's role is to direct and steer the business; to scaffold a healthy business through creating an effective culture and living the strong positive values that support business success. Typically, this is carried out through strategic planning that will give insights into the mission and vision of the business.

Regardless of management level, to be successful all managers are required to be collaborative internally and externally. A manager and leader's success will depend on forming and nurturing relationships, communication, team management, resource and time management, commercial awareness, and so much more. Kouzes and Posner (Kouzes and Posner 1987, 2010) suggest that leaders must take action to be successful and they highlight the five behaviours that are required for the leader to deliver upon to reach extraordinary results: model the way, inspire a shared vision, challenge the process, enable others to act and encourage the heart.

Executive leaders are responsible for proactive and strategic planning.

Personal reputation and brand

If you have not yet considered your personal reputation and brand, now is the time to start. Your personal reputation and brand will help or hinder your career. Your personal reputation and brand will exceed your marketing, be that your LinkedIn profile, CV, Twitter account, Facebook or other forms of marketing will take second place to word-of-mouth. Others control your personal reputation and brand; you can only influence it. You cannot insist how others perceive you. That last statement should be, and swiftly, followed by reflective time on what you would like your personal reputation and brand to represent. Quite simply, deliver to your best.

Understanding what you would like your personal reputation and brand to be allows you to consider the actions to take in order to meet them. Your personal reputation and brand are primarily about you, however, remember this and be clear around your teams' performance and behaviour; they will also be aligned to your personal reputation and brand, after all, you are their manager and are responsible for the outputs, and this includes attitude and behaviour.

If your team is performing well, and you are a good manager, your personal reputation and brand will be enhanced. If your team is performing well despite your poor management style, your personal reputation and brand will be damaged. If your team is underperforming and your reputation is poor, your personal reputation and brand will continue to be poor. If your team is underperforming in spite of you being a great manager, your personal reputation and brand will be associated with the poor team performance. At this point, you should be seeing that whilst you can influence your personal reputation and brand, it is often in the hands of others.

This reinforces the message that you need to be doing the role for you, in order to carry out with gusto and willingly delivering your best; this mindset shift will go some way towards your personal reputation and brand.

THE PERFECT MANAGER

Take the pressure off; there is no perfect manager. There are great managers, good managers and awful managers. You can take ownership and responsibility for which category you wish to align with. It would be impossible to capture all the requirements and responsibilities for a senior manager within this book. Different businesses, sectors and industries require different styles of management. The categories are often interchangeable and situational and require the manager to be flexible and confident enough to apply as required, apart from the last one, awful manager.

However, the more you receive attention for one particular label, the stronger your reputation is aligned with that label. It is difficult although not impossible once labelled a poor or underperforming manager to change or move away from this, short of moving company. Even then, your reputation will exceed your marketing.

Managers will be required to be flexible and should be prepared to engage effectively depending upon the audience and situation. A manager's style is not absolute and static; they may present a different style when presenting in front of a large group as they would presenting to a small group. A manager will present differently to a client than they would their team. Awareness of the environment and audience is key; the ability to present the effective style without conscious thought is honed over time, you will get there through practice and reflection.

A senior manager is often categorised as a middle manager; the title is interchangeable. For this book, we will work with senior manager. There is a reason that senior managers are also known as middle managers; this is due to their placement in seniority, between first-line managers and the leadership team. It can, on occasions, feel as if you as senior manager have been caught between a rock and a hard place, the reality is you will possibly be keeping one happy more so than the other at any given time.

For a senior manager, they are the direct reports of the executive leadership team, and therefore are managing the responsibilities of the strategic plan through the translation to meet company goals, whilst they are managing a team of first-line managers and the day-to-day operations of delivering on the strategic and business plan. The responsibilities don't always align.

There is no one size fits all. What works for one company in a particular industry may not work for another company in the same industry. Take the pressure off; do not strive for perfection.

This book focuses on core requirements.

Great managers, regardless of industry, will have similar attributes and similar measurements of success. However, there is no checklist. You are an individual, adopt and adapt your learning from this book to work for you.

KEY PERFORMANCE INDICATORS

Some of the measurements that I share with my development clients through coaching and group development are 'key performance indicators' (KPIs). The first is you can measure a good to great manager on how long their team can effectively and efficiently deliver when the manager is out of the office. If a manager is out of the office on a week or two weeks' holiday and the team are effective, good. If the manager is out of the office through unplanned leave and the team are effective, great. If the manager is out of the office and the team are not effective, this is a clear sign of poor management. This is true from the other angle, how long a manager can be out of the office without needing to check their emails or phone. A good to great manager will have a team who they trust to manage in their absence and to carry out their day-to-day roles and responsibilities regardless if they are there or not.

A second great KPI for a good to great manager is having an informed team who are aware of what is happening within the team and the bigger picture. A third KPI for a good to great manager is having a successor in waiting or in development to step in when you as the senior manager are out of the office, whether that be in a meeting, on holiday, or unexpected absence. You get to choose which category you wish to be aligned with. Choose wisely.

GOOD TO GREAT MANAGER ATTRIBUTES

Regardless of seniority, what great leaders and managers have in common is:

Communication

The number one attribute of any manager at any level, in fact of any employee, is communication. Effective communication often involves listening more than talking. Gaining an understanding of the other person's requirements and reason for the engagement. Then and only then delivering your communication style to suit the receiver. This may involve short and sharp, long and detailed, or delivered in advance; it should suit the style of the receiver and not you. The communication tone and pitch will be relevant to the subject and the recipient and mirroring their body language will build rapport.

Confidently giving and receiving complimentary and constructive feedback

A survey carried out by The Bute Group highlighted that 81% of employees would not re-employ their managers back into their current position, that is, 81% of survey participants do not want to work with their managers. From that 81%, three key areas of concern, 79% said they received no feedback from the manager, 46% highlighted that the manager did not delegate work to them or anyone else and 63% stated they did not receive any development.

Mature (in terms of experience and not age) managers look for the win:win in every engagement and opportunity. The win:win mindset is one where you are looking to meet both your own and the other party's requirements. When you are engaging with others, have clarity around your requirements and ask questions to understand the other party's requirements. The engagement may involve negotiation and compromise; however, it is not about you giving up your requirements, or the other party theirs, it involves both parties compromising. Without the win:win mindset, you or the other party will walk away feeling hard done by. This win:win mindset must be applied to each and every engagement, including with your team and with your manager.

Selfish managers receive minimum support from the team; if the team constantly feel as if they have been mistreated during the engagement they will start to back off and not give their best to completing your requests to the best of their ability, why would they? This same is true of your engagement with your own manager; you should be perceiving this relationship as a form of support for you. All parties involved should be looking to collaborate and work towards business success.

Your manager should be an ally and ambassador for you, and that only becomes observable when you have an authentic relationship. If the relationship isn't working, look at your input, are you focusing on the win:win? Your team are not paid to be overworked and under-recognised, and a win:win approach with them and those who you are engaging with is crucial.

The win:win truly is about all parties involved giving and taking, and each and every one walking away feeling that the engagement was fair and honest. Thus, building trust, integrity and long-term relationships, and of course, elevating your personal reputation and brand.

Feedback

Senior managers can often shy away from providing feedback, particularly those managers who are new to the role. Or if the manager is to provide constructive feedback to individuals, this can often be received as negative feedback when delivered poorly. It is important for your personal development and growth, as well as the recipient's team development growth, that you provide balanced feedback on a regular basis. Sharing constructive feedback when required is liberating, go into it with a win:win mindset.

As a senior manager you will look to ensure that unacceptable behaviours and outcomes are nipped in the bud and not repeated. Knowing what you want as an alternative to the unacceptable behaviour is your win and working with the recipient on how they will and can achieve this is their win.

Recognition for good work should also be provided. Often managers get stuck in only providing feedback focusing on the past; great feedforward (what changes or duplication you would like to see in the future) is just as important to team members in order to set direction, goals and challenges.

The feedback process, regardless of whether you perceive the conversation to be around negative issues, should always have the goal of positive change and outcomes.

Know your reason for providing feedback: is it to develop, motivate, inform, correct, praise or other?

Assertive behaviour

Great managers always focus on the win:win approach. To work with the other party to ensure that both parties walk away feeling respected and heard. They take a 'what's in it for me?' and 'what's in it for the other party?' approach.

Assertive behaviour also demonstrates the senior manager's thought through response to the many requests that they will receive; saying yes to those that support the business, team and your own goals, and no to those that take away, or is not their team's area of expertise. Being a people pleaser and never saying no will be a form of frustration to your team. Always saying yes typically transpires into your team having to work harder than what is actually required. Saying no can be a difficult transition for a manager when stepping into a senior manager's role.

It is an obvious sign of immaturity with regards to management experience when a manager, regardless of seniority, responds yes to every request. It can be difficult enough to manage your own resources without taking on the additional workload that can and should be delegated to the correct team.

Honest, fair and transparent

These values should ring true for anyone within the business, not just senior managers. Values will drive a great team culture and allow you to set boundaries. Honest managers do not knowingly misinform or lie, even on the occasions where they are unable to share information and knowledge on confidential matters with others, which may include redundancies, salary review, grievances, disciplinaries etc.

There is a difference between not sharing and being dishonest. Honest managers will decline to say anything rather than making up excuses or deception. Fair managers treat everyone the same, regardless. A process of procedure for one team member is available to all. Transparent managers instil a degree of trust and loyalty; there is a general sense of nothing to hide, you do not get involved in gossip, you do not talk about team members, your manager or anyone else in a negative manner. You are transparent; if you have a concern with a team member or other, you deal directly with the person, or seek assistance in managing the situation from your own manager, a peer, possibly HR, and carry this out professionally and respectfully.

Honest, fair and transparent are great adjectives to hear aligned with anyone's personal reputation and brand.

Approachable and flexible

Approachable senior managers will often hear and see more from their team and their direct reports. This is not an invitation to host gossip sessions or play at office politics, or becoming the in-house agony aunt or uncle. Approachable is perceived as open and professional and being flexible and appropriate where required enhances your personal reputation and brand as someone who is organised and understands the reality of business.

Hearing the terms approachable and flexible with regards to your personal reputation and brand is another great boost.

Organised

Typical changes within a promotion to a senior manager's role will include the additional responsibilities that are associated with the new role, including the management and organisation of several first-line managers that often transpires into potentially managing several teams within different disciplines. A key skill is organisation, this will give you the breathing space to stay on top whilst managing your other responsibilities. Managing your resources in an effective and efficient manner is crucial to meeting your department's goals alongside the business goals.

Meetings

Managing your own time more effectively and efficiently will become fundamental due to the ramped-up volume of meetings you will be invited to attend. The number of meetings will likely become untenable. With the new working profile (as a result of COVID-19) of primarily working from home, there is a requirement to be in regular contact with your team as the team is likely to be geographically dispersed.

There is a requirement to rate your meetings and ask, 'do I have to attend?', 'what is required of me at the meeting?', 'what will I get from attending?', 'would one of my team reports be better suited?', 'does there need to be a presence at all?'

If you decide it is you who should attend, ensure that you attend meetings on time. Have you noticed when someone is late to a meeting? Most people look at their watches, the latecomer, if consistently poor with their timekeeping, their personal reputation and brand will greatly suffer. Ringfence time to prepare for all meetings. Preparation will empower you to know when to say yes to a request and equally when to say no.

Calm and engaging

Let's be honest, regardless of position or seniority, there will always be times where you will feel stressed. A senior manager will successfully manage their emotions. They will remove themselves from toxic and stressful situations, taking the time to think through the situation calmly, and when choosing to deal with others will present themselves in a calm and engaging manner.

Day-to-day stresses happen and the exceptional stress situations. A senior manager should not present an overly emotional self; the goal is to be in a position to make logical and feasible decisions.

CHAPTER REFLECTION AND ACTION PLAN

Chapter reflections and action plans provide you with an opportunity to stop and breathe. Take time to reflect and complete the exercises.

To assist with this, you will follow Cameron's journey and how she used this book to progress her career, firstly into a senior management role and then progress and develop within the role.

CAMERON

Cameron is a fictional character and an amalgamation of many of my clients whom I observed and have worked with.

Cameron is married with two young children. Cameron's partner is also in full-time employment. She had been working in an operational role as a first-line manager for three years. Over the previous 12 months, she was looking to progress into a senior management role. It became apparent to Cameron within the current business there would be no potential to fulfil her desire for promotion. Cameron decided in the last six months to look for a new role externally.

She had looked at several job specifications online, but she wasn't sure if she was ready for a new role; some of the skills she thought she may have, some she certainly did not.

Cameron checked out the books on the market and purchased this book. Cameron used the book initially to gain a greater understanding of the role of senior manager.

She was successful in her applications and started in a senior management role in a new company. The story picks up with Cameron when she had been in the new role and company for just three weeks. She has three separate teams: operations, marketing and IT. Cameron had been a manager of an operations team in her previous company.

And so, it begins...

It was important for Cameron to gain a better understanding of her new company. Who fits where and with what? Cameron carried out an exercise based on the following:

1. Understand if the business has several levels of hierarchy or a flat hierarchical business model.

2. Within this model, have absolute clarity around where you fit in within the organisation.

3. Review both the org chart and business plan.

4. As you explore the questions, consider how you might start to network and introduce yourself to others.

5. Within your new senior management role, reflect on your personal reputation and brand and what you want people to be saying about you when you are not in the room; this is your personal reputation. Reflect on what you want others to be saying about your delivery; this is your brand.

6. Note this down in a conversation format and not just short bullet points.

It is important for Cameron's success and confidence that she understands the busines she is operating within. Cameron's new company has several layers of management, and therefore she sourced an organisation chart. It was clear where she sat within the organisation and who would be in the senior management team.

Cameron listed her answers down alongside her thoughts on what she would like her personal reputation and brand to represent. She would refer to these notes at a later date.

YOUR TURN...

Time for you to carry out the above exercise. Take your time.

CHAPTER 1

ALIGN YOUR MOTIVATIONS TO YOUR CAREER ASPIRATIONS

Quite simply, if you are required or need to carry out anything of worth in both your personal and professional life, know your own why, know your own motivators. It has to be about you.

It is the 'good deed' part of being human to carry out work for other individuals, and on occasions even to do things that we would rather not be doing for someone else, and we often do that within our day-to-day work environment. However, if you only conduct your career choices because others want you to be in that position, with that status, earning that salary, driving that car, and buying that house, it may be a struggle to carry out with a sense of energy, enjoyment and authenticity. It is important for your own wellbeing that you consider your wants, wishes and own your career choices and ambition.

YOUR AMBITION

Your family, friends and partner will always (or at least should) want the best for you and your career is likely to be included in this. Within the work environment, status is often measured on your title and remuneration package. It is not unusual to want to be the person that others want you to be. Having others as your cheerleaders can be motivational. However, it can also be physically and mentally draining when you aspire to be the person that others want you to be whilst you want to be doing something entirely different.

Management roles are particularly seen as being successful; frequently, with management roles comes a new title, enhanced salary and rewards, additional authority and responsibilities, etc. In a nutshell, a greater status. These roles can, on occasions, be lonely and isolating, and if this is not your ambition, if this is not what you want to be, if this isn't in the career trajectory that you were looking for, it can be soul-destroying.

Your need to understand and acknowledge your ambition is a must; whilst money is a good driver, it is often not the main driver, it is a means to an end. If money is a key driver (it is for a lot of people), you will find money comes easier when you are passionate and enjoying your role. Just chasing the big bucks can be demoralising.

Titles are great for ego boosts but they do not sustain personal happiness; responsibility can be energising but it doesn't create an energy that is not ready to be ignited; challenges can be rewarding if they are challenges that you are ready to conquer but it doesn't conjure up enthusiasm. When carrying out a role as part of the career you want and are striving for, it is easier to apply the energy to understanding the needs of the business, and with enthusiasm, you can gauge your capabilities and limitations on the delivery required.

You will be motivated to develop yourself through reading, development programmes, coaching and mentoring, YouTube, following relevant groups and influencers and networking with the right people. This enthusiasm, confidence and knowledge will transpire into you authentically caring that you and your team are delivering to at least meet business requirements, and where appropriate to exceed business requirements. This will feed your ambition.

The alternative is you don't genuinely care about your career, and you are going through the motions until you become a statistic on the 'Peter principle'. This being that managers are promoted based on their current levels of competence and will continue to be promoted until they reach their 'level of incompetence'. The reality for most managers in this position is that they have become so caught up in the work and proving themselves that they have forgotten about their own ambitions and therefore have taken their foot off the pedal of their own development.

It is an important mindset that individuals are accountable for their own development; they do not rely solely on their employers to meet their development requirements. For most of my career, I have allocated a minimum of 10% of my net salary to development, on occasions accumulating that 10% over years and then allocating it to a career-changing development programme. The sense of achievement is indescribable to be responsible for your career and making it happen.

It is OK to change course through your career. I hope that you are in the role that you chose and worked towards, and therefore you may jump between industries and sectors, you may jump between departments, and you may even change disciplines. The important part is that you make the conscious decision, you own the course of change, and it propels you in the direction that you wish to be journeying on. Acknowledge and thank others for their ambitions and support of you; however, be sure too that you are taking the career path that you want.

You can give yourself a pat on the back; by reading this book you are developing your senior manager muscles. Own it.

CURRENT ROLE

We all have times even when we are carrying out a role that we love when we feel demotivated and underwhelmed. There may be many reasons for this; you will consider two…

The first, it may be time to move on to your next set of challenges and rewards. You have learned what you can and given what you had of this role. This is a great place, stop, breathe and feel the satisfaction that you have outgrown the role and delivered well within it.

The second is that the role is not right for you. You have given it your best; it is simply not the right fit. This is a great place, stop, breathe and feel the satisfaction that you recognised this and can take action, whilst identifying and being thankful for the learnings you can take away from the experience.

You have picked this book up for a reason, what is the primary reason? This book will support your development within or moving into a senior manager role.

"I AM WORTH THE INVESTMENT"

I would like you to repeat the heading several times, and if you can repeat it out loud without disturbing those around you then do so, or repeat to yourself, "I am worth the investment", "I am worth the investment", "I am worth the investment", "I am worth the investment."

In the earlier paragraph you will have taken away the absolute need to have clarity around your motivators, not least so that you can influence your personal reputation and brand in the right direction, and this will feed into your ambition and career.

The investment that you have made in this book in terms of purchasing and allocating the time to read and complete the exercises will reap many benefits. The level of investment that you make in terms of reflection, planning and execution will be returned 10-fold. You are worth the investment; you are worth setting the time aside to reflect, consider and action your career. Make the decision now and ringfence time in your calendar to deliver on you. You are worth it.

KNOW YOUR SKILL SET AND CAPABILITIES

Most people, at some point in their career, will have completed an appraisal with their manager, or you may even have been the appraiser in the engagement. The primary principles of an appraisal process are that the appraisee carries out self-reflection and notes their self-perceived performance to date, they receive feedback on their past performance from the appraiser (typically their manager) which includes an update on the successes and a warm and glowing reference to their behaviour and outcome, followed by a look at their limitations and discussion around development. There is a clear understanding of the appraisee's requirements and targets for the coming year. For you, as the appraisee, you gain a greater understanding of where you align your focus for the successive 12 months.

With or without the input of others, it will be fundamental to your success to understand what your career ambitions look and feel like. Having clarity around how you will measure your success: will this be measured in terms of job title? Remuneration? Internal or external promotions? Responsibilities? Or other? Understanding this will allow you to start researching the requirements of your next role and compare the requirements to where you are in terms of current abilities, attitude and behaviour versus what will be required and expected of you.

Just in case you don't believe this to be true as yet, repeat once more, "I am worth the investment."

FEELING LIKE A FRAUD, THE IMPOSTER SYNDROME

There is a rise in managers acknowledging out loud that they feel as if they don't deserve their jobs, that they are impostors and are going to be found out at any time. That fear is hanging over them like a dark cloud. Acknowledgement of this fear is on the increase, and there are a greater number of managers who are addressing the issue.

Imposter syndrome has stopped many moving on from their roles and the thought of going for a promotion strikes fear in their hearts. Without exception, each and every one of us will feel this at some stage in our career. Be prepared for this to creep up on you, or if you are feeling this currently, this is wholly unjustified, and it is often the fear of failing that places people in this mindset state. Through reflection and action, this can be overcome.

You have got this. "I am worth the investment!"

Are you an imposter?

You are in a role and don't feel as if you deserve to be there, and this may be for a number of reasons. You feel your age is against you, too old or too young. You do not have the experience for the role, possibly lack qualifications, or you are managing a colleague who would be better suited to the role as they have worked there longer and therefore know the business better. You, the imposter, may believe that you don't deserve the salary, (the salary leap from your previous role is vast). You may feel you have been promoted too quickly and your new position is too senior for your abilities.

Then there's the feeling of being out of control, when you feel you can't manage and you're plunged into some situations expecting to fail, you feel you do not have the knowledge to back up any questions should you be asked, everyone else knows better, everyone expects you to be the expert. These and more lead from the fear of humiliation, of being found out, then the fear of rejection, of being sacked; the fear of the pain caused to self and others from the perceived deception.

Now start to look at your behaviour, are you frozen with fear? Over compensating? Being . very assertive (read aggressive), deflecting the blame on to others, and the list goes on. If only you had stayed where you were... when will you be found out?

Can you relate to this?

Genuine article

There are ways that this could be tackled. The very first thing anyone who is in this position and is suffering imposter syndrome should do is to stop and breathe.

Find a couple of hours in your calendar and dedicate this to start addressing the fear and eradicating the label of the imposter.

Stop and breathe. "I am worth the investment." At the beginning of the allotted time, stop and breathe for a couple of minutes. Stop and breathe. "I am worth the investment." Stop and breathe. "I am worth the investment."

And now that you are in a state of feeling more relaxed and prepared, you are ready to address the problem and consider the options.

Stop procrastinating and take action!

It is time to put an end to the toxic thoughts and responses.

Gain a greater understanding of your current role. If you are currently in a senior management role, choosing to stay in the role will give you an opportunity to address the problem head-on. This will potentially trigger a series of events, with positive outcomes. This could be the start of facing your insecurities head-on and coming out of this stronger and more capable. What a boost this will be to your confidence and brand.

Why did you get the role?

Even if you believe it was only because you were in the right place at the right time (or the wrong place at the wrong time), there would have been something about you that attracted the decision-makers to appoint you to the role. What was that? What did you have? Experience? A great understanding of the business? Different viewpoint from others? Did you demonstrate managerial skills? Were you keen to show your potential? What was it? There was something. Stop and breathe.

If you are moving into a new role or preparing to apply for a new role, consider what you can bring to the table; for this exercise, focus on the positives.

TASKS AND RESPONSIBILITIES

What does the role require?

Now you have a better idea of why you were selected for the role. Consider what the role entails. What skill sets are required? Which behaviours will be required to be successful within the role? What are the measurable outcomes that your success will be measured on? What are the essential outcomes that you are being measured on? What are the desirables of the role?

What are your strengths?

From the above, which skills and behaviours have you already nailed? Which other strengths can you bring to the role? Focus on your strengths only; it is vital to remain realistic at this stage.

Consider which strengths would your best friend say you have? What feedback on your strengths would your favourite boss tell you? What feedback would your least favourite boss tell you? List these and then match to the role requirements. What other strengths will support your success?

What areas require development?

Be realistic with this list. This is probably easier to identify due to your state of mind. Remember, at this point you are working towards balance. Consider what your best friend would say if you asked what your limitations are. What would your favourite boss tell you? And your least favourite boss? List these. Match these to the role requirements.

Your focus here is to get balanced feedback. *Crazy thought, would it actually be worth asking for feedback?*

WHERE DO YOU NEED TO FOCUS YOUR DEVELOPMENT?

You now have a list of role requirements where you can support these requirements and areas at required development. Within the development range, which are the priorities? Which are desirable? This is your area of focus.

Support

Balance is key in the exercise. Support will bring balance. If appropriate, work with your manager on this and if not your manager, do you have a mentor? How about a coach? Having someone who will support you and engage you without judgment is vital. A supporter who will work with you on a plan of action and work with you on your success. Someone who can help you focus your attention on the bigger picture to bring balance, results, outcomes and be a sounding board and more. Consider someone who will respectfully provide kind challenges to your thoughts and plans; the challenges often provide the greatest 'aha' moments.

There are alternatives to the above.

Resign or stay put and do nothing

If you are reading this book to enhance your mindset and skill set as an existing senior manager; the most obvious and easiest course of action to take when you are suffering from imposter syndrome is to resign before you are caught out or make a mistake. Resign before you are asked the question you do not know the answer to. Resign before you are sacked. Resign before the humiliation.

If you're reading this book to prepare yourself for the step up into a senior management role and don't feel you are worthy of that, then stay put, stay in your current role. Consider the joy and safety net that this will provide, do nothing other than worry and grow even more anxious.

These are not the ideal actions

Choosing to resign or do nothing will trigger a series of events, potentially all with negative outcomes. Including resigning from all future jobs, as your confidence takes a major dip every time you choose to resign or make no changes. It will feel as if everyone else is moving forward and you're not, which won't just be a feeling, it will be factual. A grave concern around this thought pattern is that the company will be moving forward to stay relevant, and there is a real requirement that you will have to move with the times, or alternatively, move to smaller and less progressive companies. With lack of development, your salary will remain static. And of course, pessimism will seep into all areas of your life, not just your work.

Believe me, this is not a sustainable long-term plan. The fact that you are reading this book should tell you that you are ready to take the necessary steps to develop yourself within your existing role and prepare for your next move.

Repeat after me, "I am worth the investment."

PERCEIVED CHALLENGES

Time to take action against imposter syndrome and be accountable for your next steps and development.

What do you believe are the challenges that you are facing? Is it that you don't know what to do? Is it that you are not prepared? Is it that your business acumen in the area is not strong? Whatever the challenges that you perceive, there will be a workaround. There are methodologies and frameworks that will support you in overcoming these challenges.

A lot of challenges will be imaginary, although feel very real to you. A lot of the barriers that you put in front of you can easily be overcome or will be non-existent. I am in no way demeaning those challenges or barriers; there will be some that are genuinely in place and difficult, you need to have absolute clarity around what is a genuine challenge and what is a perceived challenge.

KNOWING WHERE YOU NEED TO BE AND HOW

New jobs, regardless of whether you are stepping up or in situ, should be challenging. If you have moved into a role that doesn't challenge you, it simply means that you have stepped into your previous role or taken a sidestep. I repeat, new roles should be challenging; there should be a degree of not knowing and feeling challenged; new roles should feel like there is a requirement for development.

When considering a new role, compare your fit to the requirements; if this is a new role or you are looking to step into a new role, it should not be a 100% fit. A good rule of thumb (a rule that I've applied personally within my career) is that when you stop learning and growing within your existing role, it is time to consider your next move.

When comparing your existing capabilities to any new role requirements, if the existing fit is less than 50%, it is still doable, the challenge will be greater and the time span to bridge the gap longer. Prioritisation is the name of the game: what would be the essential skill set required to step into the new role? How do you bridge the gap from where you are to where you are required to be? Which task would give you the quickest win? Which task could you carry out that would give you a deeper learning experience? Which task could you carry out that will give you a wider reach? Consider the return on investment for you having put in the preparation work to enable the career that you want. If the existing fit is 50-75%, this is less of a challenge, and possibly, there will be a learning curve, not a steep one. If the existing fit is 75-100%, this is a sideways move.

Repeat after me, "I am worth the investment."

PROMOTION LEADS TO ADDITIONAL REWARDS

The wonderful part of promotions is the additional rewards; these rewards may be both tangible and non-tangible rewards. Tangible is relatively easy to measure: salary increase, employee rewards, private healthcare, enhanced pension scheme, status and more. And whilst these are clearly of importance, it will be the non-tangible rewards, your true motivators, that will get you out of bed in the early morning and keep you up later in the evening, it will be these motivators that you bring to mind when you need that extra oomph.

These rewards should and will drive your motivation to bridge the gap between what is required and where you are currently. Know your motivators – your motivators not anyone else's. For the tangible returns, research market rates, know what the benchmark is for your next role, understand the market drivers, where is the power, supply or demand? Acknowledge the impact that this change will have on your career and on your life in general.

LOOKING FOR A FREE RIDE?

Few companies will give you a free ride; the greater the reward, the greater the expectation is on return on investment, and therefore this will be measured in terms of your delivery. For you, that will involve a greater motivation for you to want to give more of yourself. The law of balance comes into play here in its absolute best when you take with one hand you give with the other. An example of this will often be the greater the salary, the greater the expectation of your availability.

For some companies, the expectation here is that you will make yourself available at all times, during holidays, weekends and evenings. The law of balance demonstrates that by taking on the additional responsibility and the additional rewards you give more of your time and availability. If you are carrying out the role for your reasons, this may make the trade-off more palatable. If you are carrying out the role to please others, you may find that the trade-off is not worth it and that you feel resentful. Know and own your motivation.

CONSIDER THE INDUSTRY AND THE EMPLOYER

Remind yourself of your personal reasons for choosing to be in a senior management role and being good and great at it. Another consideration is which companies you would like to be associated with. Are you prepared to work with companies that have links directly and indirectly with creating and supporting wars? Advocating tobacco and alcohol? Large drug companies? Companies associated with poor employee treatment and more? Are you looking to work with charitable foundations? The financial sector? What are you prepared to give and take? This is about your wants and wishes and knowing what meets your needs. This decision will be of great importance to your personal reputation and brand.

Consider the culture of a company, is it one that you would like to be associated with? This consideration can be career enhancing as well is career limiting. Honouring your values is fundamental to your wellbeing and understanding the true values of a company will allow you to decide whether you wish to work there or not. Those values that are often displayed on meeting room windows and kitchen posters are not always the values that are being observed and demonstrated within a company. Spend some time researching the company's culture and values before making a final decision on whether to apply or accept a job offer.

For the final time in this chapter repeat after me "I am worth the investment."

CHAPTER REFLECTION AND ACTION PLAN

Understanding your personal reasons for wanting the promotion or enhancing your capability with the new current role will be a greater driver than working to meet someone else's wants and wishes for you, even when the intentions of the other person are well intended. There is strong emphasis on you being the driver of your career, and firstly determining whether this is yours or another's, be that of a partner, family or friend's wants and desires. Understanding your personal drivers will take you further than trying to meet someone else's aspirations of you. For a long-term commitment to your career, you must understand your reasons for this. Your personal reasons will willingly get you out of bed early in the morning and keep you up late at night to get the job done. The need to put in the extra hours will become more difficult, and you may even resent what you're doing and the others for placing the level of responsibility on you.

Understand your personal reasons for wanting this promotion and developing yourself.

CAMERON

Cameron has always had career aspirations. As her family grew, she wanted to provide for them even more. Her parents and partner are proud to tell people that she is a senior manager in the finance industry. In particular that she is working for a company that is growing with plans for global expansion.

Cameron thought she owned her choices; however, she chose to take the time to complete the exercises.

On completing this chapter, Cameron had clarity around her career aspirations. She took the time to reflect on her passions and wishes. She reflected back to the earlier questions in this chapter and answered them, and then completed the exercise below. She found the exercise difficult at times as she was being very honest (possibly for the first time) around her motivations. On reflection, she realised she wanted the promotion and the challenges.

Whilst in an ideal world she would be working from home as a trader, and giving some time to her favourite charities, the reality is she has never pursued this passion. She enjoys the security of a monthly salary.

Cameron decided in her next move she would research charitable businesses as this may suit her. Cameron is very aware of the income requirements to contribute to the family lifestyle and household. This new role meets her needs and more, and Cameron is happy with this. She realised as she carried out the exercise that she was good at her job, and whilst she didn't know everything, who does?

YOUR TURN...

The following exercise is the first step in this:

1. Reflect on where you are in your career.
2. If you are where you wish to be, how did you get to this place?
3. If you have been overlooked for promotions, what do you believe is missing? What feedback have you evidenced this on?
4. Why do YOU want to be a senior manager? You can, of course, include external reasons, to provide for your family etc.

Please remember all roads must lead back to your wants and wishes to become a great senior manager.

CHAPTER 2

MANAGING YOUR WORKING STYLES, RESPONSES AND BEHAVIOURS

In this chapter you will continue to reflect and consider you. A key understanding of yourself is to recognise your preferred working styles. Preferred working styles are styles that you carry out without thought; it's the style that you revert to when the pressure is on and it is comfortable, not carried out consciously as the styles are so intrinsic in your day-to-day thinking and behaviour. These styles are like a comfort blanket, a go-to style that takes no thinking or effort to deliver.

Young managers, and again, I use the term 'young' in measurement of experience as opposed to age, often at a conscious and unconscious level will mirror their own manager's styles, particularly, if they see their manager getting results. If their manager's style fits in with the culture of the company, their working styles are rewarded and their manager receives recognition from the senior leadership team, then surely the thought process would be this works, why would I not copy it?

Utilising a style frequently enough develops to the unconscious competence stage and becomes a preferred style, a style that is habitual and without thought. A one size fits all style does not work; managers regardless of seniority are required to adapt and have flexibility when working with their styles depending on who their audience is and the situation they are presented with.

It is your responsibility to get the best out of your teams and in most instances, adapt to the team's preferred working styles where this proves effective and efficient. Do not hold any expectations that individuals will or should modify their style to match yours; they may not have received any development or read books on this area. In addition to modifying your style to match your audience and situation, it is understanding how to deliver this when engaging many people at the same time, e.g. team meetings, presentations and the like.

There are many online 'working styles' questionnaires and evaluations on the market. As at today, when typing 'working styles' in Google, it responded with 253,000,000 results. You are not asked to remember and list the 253,000,000 results.

The Bute Group (full disclosure and transparency, I am a director at The Bute Group) when working with 'working styles' place their attention on three key areas:

first, management styles, secondly, learning, and third, communication styles. Developing your knowledge of the various working styles in order to recognise them being demonstrated in others and knowing your preferred styles will allow you to ultimately evaluate in real time the effectiveness of each style based on your audience and situation.

Focus on working styles is typically discussed in detail at first-line manager's level, and for this reason, the following is a recap. It would be remiss to not mention this as it is important that you, as a senior manager, understand your style and the impact it has on others.

Most managers have a preferred style that they like to work within. You will have a natural style you prefer, a style that you do not think about, your go-to style. There will be other styles that bring you outside of your comfort zone and will need to be thought through in order to carry them out successfully. DATA© management styles will give you the framework to consider realistically which style will get the best for your team and the outcome.

Focus on three of the four styles: Affiliative, Authoritative and Transformational.

Your aim should never be to work within the disengaged manager style. As a new or young (in terms of experience) manager, you may find it difficult to recognise the styles. You may also find it uncomfortable to adapt your mindset between the three styles, and this is perfectly normal.

For now, the focus is on when and where to use the different styles. Which style will work best for which scenario?

The best way to carry this out is through reflection. Be realistic with this: you will get it wrong at times, the errors will decrease as time goes on. Remember, it is less of a mistake if you can take and implement the learnings.

The four management styles that we will focus on in this book are:

AFFILIATIVE MANAGER

For the most part, this is an emotionally rewarding style to work within, the idea being that your team comes before everything else. You ensure that your team is well taken care of. You fight their every battle, aim to ensure they are always happy, this can often be to the detriment of providing a great product or service to your clients. The team will rarely have an opportunity to take calculated risks, learn from their mistakes or anyone else's.

Occasions you may want to wear this hat is at 1:1s, team meetings and informal networking and gatherings.

AUTHORITARIAN MANAGER

Their primary concerns (often only concern) is the delivery and the outcomes of tasks. The authoritarian manager's key focus is delivering on what has been agreed; they may overdeliver on expected outcomes, believing they are delivering additional value and greater impact to the customer. They drive the department forward with a clear understanding of how and what the team should be working towards, and the results of the outcomes are measurable. It is clear whether success has been achieved, and failure to deliver is not an option. It is a command and direct approach, do it their way or the highway.

The authoritarian manager does not place much emphasis on the team's personal needs, e.g. development, workloads, etc., instead focusing all their attention on doing whatever is necessary to deliver on the agreed outcome. Therefore, they work very well with service level agreements and time-bound outcomes and goals. There is often no room for engagement for team members with the authoritarian manager. The authoritarian manager is often too focused on the need to deliver, and in their opinion, they know best how to carry this out.

Occasions you may want to wear this hat is when introducing new legislation, when a task is time sensitive, or when you have repeatedly asked for something and you have not received the outcome you wished for.

TRANSFORMATIONAL MANAGER

The transformational manager is the ideal of the four styles to work within as they take a 360° approach to their team and tasks. The transformational manager will be aware of the necessity to be flexible and work with confidence through concerns and issues without sabotaging either the task or support for their team. This comes with experience: it cannot be bought or borrowed.

Occasions you may wish to wear this hat, ideally, you may be thinking always, however, the reality is impossible to sustain. Do not set yourself up for failure or undue stress by aiming to continuously and only work within this style.

DISENGAGED MANAGER

Oh, what a treat this manager is to work for. The disengaged manager cares about nothing and no one. They like to delegate tasks and full responsibility regardless of the individual's knowledge or ability and do not care about the tasks or their team. The disengaged manager is possibly a great game player, but not an honest or authentic manager, and certainly not likeable.

This is not a style to which you ever aspire.

PERSONAL VALUES

You have read about values in earlier chapters; your values will be a key influence in your working style and behaviour. Your values can be defined as your strong beliefs on correct standards, conduct and outcomes. When you are working in a company where you are feeling positively challenged, receiving the opportunity to learn every day, are happy and content (for the most part) then you have found a company whose values match your own.

The opposite is true when you are working in an organisation where you are in a constant state of anger, stress and your wellbeing is suffering as a result; there is a high possibility that you and the company have diametrically opposing values.

Recognising and honouring your values is important for your wellbeing. Consider a time when you were really happy? Proud? Angry? Ask yourself why? The answer may give you insight into a strong value that was being honoured or dishonoured.

Shalom H. Schwartz, psychologist and renowned for his research and creation of the 'Theory of basic human values', highlights 10 values:

1. Self-direction – independent thinking and goal setting.

2. Stimulation – enjoys a challenging and exciting life.

3. Hedonism – enjoys a pleasurable life.

4. Achievement – personal and perceived success, ambitious, capable and more.

5. Power – social status and recognition, control and authority.

6. Security – stability in all areas of life, e.g. family, relationships, society.

7. Conformity – works within social norms, not one to upset the cart.

8. Tradition – respectful of traditions and where one sits within this.

9. Benevolence – helpful and responsible for others' wellbeing.

10. Universalism – social justice, appreciation and tolerance for all.

Whilst you may not recognise all of these within your own personal values, they are a guideline on where your values may (not should) lie. Do not worry, if your values are not clear, you will start to recognise them through time and reflection. Some of your values will change over time; however, your core values will remain unwavering throughout life; at the very least, the core values are worth exploring.

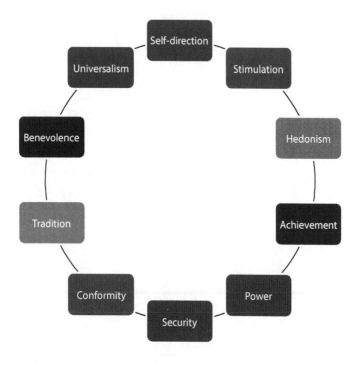

(Adapted from Schwartz, 1992)

EMOTIONAL INTELLIGENCE

I am very cautious about using the term 'intelligence' in my writing and speaking. It almost always conjures up associations around academic intelligence. And for some, academic education was not their route into business. I personally believe that academic intelligence demonstrates that you can remember and repeat. I am in no way demeaning academic intelligence or qualifications; I believe those who hold these qualifications demonstrate key attributes that are vital to business and personal success. What I would like to highlight is that academic intelligence is not the only form of intelligence. Howard Gardner presents nine types of intelligence (Gardner 2008):

1. Naturalistic Intelligence – nature smart

2. Musical Intelligence – music smart

3. Logical-Mathematical Intelligence – reasoning and number smart

4. Existential Intelligence – spiritual smart

5. Interpersonal Intelligence – people and social smart

6. Bodily-Kinaesthetic Intelligence – body smart

7. Linguistic Intelligence – word smart

8. Intrapersonal Intelligence – self smart

9. Visual-Spatial Intelligence – picture and space smart

The above 'smarts' (often learned outside of the academic environment) are not often measured in an academic environment; it is important to recognise your own and others' intelligences and smarts outside traditional academic thinking, and respect and honour them as a strength. If you were to reflect on additional categories, what would you add to Gardner's list of intelligences? Do not place people in boxes; everyone has hidden talents that they or others don't recognise. A great senior manager will gently coax these out of their team individuals and self.

This above list omits emotional intelligence (EI), also referred to as EI and EQ (emotional quotient). EI is just as vital; within the real world some may say even more valuable than academic intelligence. Daniel Goleman is a world-class author who brought emotional intelligence into the business platform through his 1995 New York Times bestseller *Emotional Intelligence*. Goleman identified five key components of emotional intelligence: "Self-awareness, Self-regulation, Motivation, Empathy and Social Skills. Understanding your level of emotional intelligence will be vital to your success. Mastering each of the five components will make all aspects of your life simpler. The order of the components is key; each one is interconnected and builds on from the previous. Therefore, mastering self-awareness followed by self-regulation and then motivation, empathy and social skills is the order that would be ideal; however, the reality is as you strengthen one, the others will naturally get stronger; they are symbiotic." (Goleman 2009).

The following are recommendations that you could consider within the work environment (although this exercise is transferable across all aspects of your life).

SELF-AWARENESS

Within the business environment, self-awareness is having a greater understanding of your moods, the emotional responses to these and your 'hot buttons' associated with individuals and situations. Your hot buttons will be your instant and without thought responses and behaviours to individuals and situations that trigger instant moods, emotions and responses without much or any prodding required.

Emotional intelligence is having the awareness to recognise your responses. Through empirical research, I have observed managers' responses to different situations.

The first, when a manager had not received the requested outcome from a direct report, they responded angrily. This manifested in various ways, predominantly through communication either in outright anger, passive-aggressiveness or monosyllabic curt responses.

A second scenario I repeatedly observed has been managers retreating to the desk to lick their wounds having received what they perceived as negative feedback from their manager. Their manager perceived this behaviour as immature.

A third scenario has been managers responding in an overly positive manner to what has been a serious situation, underperformance or delivery. An example of this was when a manager responded with, "Let's not dwell on this, let's put this behind us and move forward, we can get up and running quickly, there is no need to discuss and draw this out", delivered in an unauthentic upbeat tone and pitch, in response to their team being reduced by 50% through redundancies.

Self-awareness extends beyond your response to a situation; it includes understanding the impact of those responses on this situation and the individuals involved. It includes having self-confidence, being realistic with your expectations on yourself; it helps in this self-assessment component to include being able to laugh at yourself by not taking yourself too seriously.

SELF-REGULATION

Self-regulation regulates your response and impact. Being self-aware of the response offers you the opportunity to regulate those responses.

Scenario 1, manager responds inappropriately to not receiving what they had requested. They are annoyed, responding in a non-productive manner, e.g. angrily or passive-aggressively. This response currently does not motivate the team member to produce something better next time, nor does it satisfy the manager's need.

THE IMPACT

It instils a culture of fear; your team will be fearful of your response if they do not get the request correct. This fear eats away at the recipient's confidence and causes additional stress that, in turn, creates an environment where even more mistakes are made.

THINKING BEFORE EXECUTING YOUR RESPONSE

Scenario 2, regulating your response to answer in a level-headed manner would be more appropriate. Initially, this involves taking some time between receiving the below-par offering to addressing it, giving yourself time to think through and deal with the anger. Through repeated use of this step, the time between receiving the below-par offering to addressing it will reduce greatly until you are in a position to self-regulate your response and deal with the issue in real time, i.e. at time of delivery.

You are, of course, allowed to be angry, annoyed and upset; however, within the professional environment and also within a personal environment responding negatively to this does not do anyone any favours, least of all you; consider what this means to your personal reputation and brand. What will the receiver of this negative response be saying about you when you are not in the room? Include within the reflection who the recipient is sharing the negative experience with... your personal reputation and brand exceeds your marketing.

Sulking, as in scenario 1, highlights a level of immaturity; this is what you may expect from children, not a manager within the business environment.

Give yourself time to regulate your response by suggesting to your manager that you reflect on the feedback and regroup at a later date and time to discuss in more detail. Again, through the continued use of this step, the time between receiving negatively perceived feedback and positively self-regulating your response will reduce until you can effectively manage the situation in real time. This would include thanking the manager for the feedback, asking for further information on the concern, issue or topic and calmly talking through and agreeing on a preferred behaviour and outcome. Win:win.

The third scenario with the overly positive and unauthentic response to what could be perceived as a devastating situation, a team losing 50% of their teammates. This will have a detrimental impact on the team's emotional and physical wellbeing as they adjust to the loss of their colleagues and the new expectation that they will absorb the additional workload. The drop in motivation and productivity will be tangible.

As a manager regulating your response to be appropriate to the situation, it would have been more supportive to acknowledge the loss of the team due to redundancy, allow the team to work through this, holding team meetings to deliver group messages, give direction and updates and to set upcoming targets, whilst holding 1:1s to allow time for individuals to discuss the impact and the way forward. This may have brought the team round to a more productive place quicker than ignoring the devastation within the team. Acknowledging that people will be upset, annoyed, fearful for their own jobs, and as a result of this, motivation and productivity will drop (temporarily) would be an appropriate response rather than trying to be upbeat and sweep the situation under the carpet.

Strengthen your ability to step back, breathe and think about your reaction before you act it out; control your impulses, redirect your moods or at least manage them so that you can release them in a safe environment. Be comfortable with you, be proud of you and your ability to be open without rash and harsh judgments of yourself or others. Extend this comfort to being open to change and difference of opinions and trust in your integrity to deliver this with maturity and professionalism.

Motivation

It would be near on impossible to sustain high levels of motivation all day every day in the workplace. The unexpected happens, changes are implemented that you may not be fully on board with or expecting; you didn't get the salary increase you were expecting, someone else received the promotion you went for... Life outside of work is not always great. You will have a dip in your motivation depending on the complexity and depth of the issue; it may even take your motivation to the ground and of course this will impact your work rate.

Motivation involving recalling why you want to be in this role is crucial at these times. Refer to your action plan from the previous chapter 'Know your motivations for your career aspirations'. Remind yourself why you are reading this book, your passion and drive are greater than money or status, although this may be a key driver. Restoke your enthusiasm and energy for your career, use this motivation to see the negative cause of the loss of motivation as an opportunity to learn and reframe the loss or failure as a positive, find your motivation and move forward. Own your reasons, keep reminding yourself of your wants and wishes to rekindle goals and objectives, and motivate your sense of achievement, energy and drive.

EMPATHY

Empathy doesn't mean agreement. Having the ability to understand another's emotional state is a skill worth nurturing. Knowing and responding authentically and honestly to this will gain you a level of respect that is only given when the other person feels they have been heard, understood and respected. Within the workplace, this is understanding how a team member may feel about a decision; they may be elated or crushed, you recognise this, acknowledge it and give the individual time and consideration to deal with the emotion, this will be returned ten-fold. Consider how this will strengthen your relationship with your team. This will give you a greater understanding of the diversity and multicultural sensitivities within your team and the business.

Expanding your reach as well as your personal reputation and brand will require networking whilst strengthening new and existing relationships. Mastering this component will play a large part in this. You will work with colleagues who are like you and some who are very different. A great senior manager will actively promote diversity and differences of opinions even when not in agreement with them.

SOCIAL SKILLS

Social skills circle around your ability to communicate with others. Having a genuine desire and expertise in managing your relationships authentically and respectfully regardless of the other party's skills or situation is vital. Taking time out to listen respectfully and engage with the other party will pay dividends. Building rapport through finding mutual ground is a great start. These social skills will give you the impetus to manage larger groups effectively, keeping in mind that senior managers often manage more than one team and department. Your effectiveness in building and leading your team, influencing your manager and the business whilst leading them to success through change and crisis, is of equal importance and pivotal around your social skills.

Mastering each component becomes easier and quicker and eventually becomes habitual through practice.

Knowing what style your audience is presenting to you will allow you to respond effectively. Again, you could Google effective communication and learning styles and get thousands of returns. At The Bute Group we keep it simple with four, welcome to STEP© Styles. The following is a brief introduction to these, understanding which each one represents will allow you to respond effectively.

THE SCHOLAR

The Scholar finds comfort in research. The Scholar will want to know what are the existing processes, methods, theories and tools amongst other pieces. The Scholar places a lot of emphasis on the calibre of materials and these ideally will be written by a Scholar and peer reviewed for additional clarity.

THE THINKER

The Thinker finds comfort in having the time to think through the task in hand or the question being asked before any form of demonstrative action is required. The Thinker typically does not like to be the centre of attention and prefers to take the back seat. They are usually quiet and are good listeners.

THE ENERGISER

The Energiser is at their happiest when they are active. They thrive on new and unknown tasks. Repetition doesn't work for them. They are typically high-energy individuals who enjoy being the centre of attention. They will take on new tasks with relish, however, don't expect them to read instructions. They usually talk more than listen.

THE PRACTICALIST

The Practicalist finds comfort in the practical side of work. They enjoy interactive exercises and trialing and work with a process or task before going live. Whilst they respect the academia and theories, they prefer to be working in an environment where they can prove success through practical application.

CHAPTER REFLECTION AND ACTION PLAN

Regardless of your seniority or how junior you may be, your success will depend on how aware you are of your working styles, responses and behaviour. This chapter focuses on recognising the different working styles including emotional intelligence.

CAMERON

Cameron was unclear on her own working styles; to be honest, she had not given it much thought. She recalled a one-day training session years ago where she thinks it may have been touched upon; it hadn't resonated with her at the time. She decided to investigate and reflect further on her styles and completed an online evaluation. The results showed she had a very strong preference towards 'affiliative' management style. She recognised that she would need to balance this out with the more task-based style of 'authoritarian'. Whilst she would never want this to be her prominent style, she could see that she often took a softer approach to tasks and focused more on keeping her team happy. In the past this had resulted in deadline panics and her team would on occasion deliver to a lesser standard than she had hoped for.

She spoke with family and friends around her emotional intelligence and thought from this she was OK. However, she did see a pattern appear around 'self-awareness', she would go quiet and not address issues she was unhappy with, she was known to sulk. She started to explore 'self-regulation', what were her hot buttons, and when did this happen.

She also was overly empathic. This she knew, she had a fear of upsetting people and would take the easy route of working to support others before her own needs. She started to note this, and she tied this into her very strong preference towards 'affiliative' management style. Things were starting to make sense.

Cameron completed the following exercises.

OVER TO YOU...

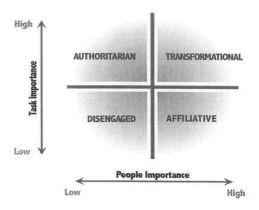

(The Bute Group, 2021)

1. Reflecting on the above graphic, within the role of senior manager list the recurring tasks you currently carry out or delegate to your team.

2. From the list, in which quartile would you place each of the tasks?

3. The tasks that you have or will delegate, how will you adapt the management style to suit you?

4. Emotional intelligence, when you master Goleman's five components, what difference will this make to your management style?

5. As you consider your 'hot buttons', consider when you last lost your temper or were angry. Complete the following: What was the trigger? What were the immediate thoughts surrounding this? What was the preceding behaviour? What would you do differently next time?

CHAPTER 3

STOP FIREFIGHTING AND LIVING IN THE DRAMA

Be afraid, very afraid, you being helpful may lead to a detrimental drop in your personal reputation and brand.

There will be times in your career, certainly in your senior management role, I suspect before today and definitely going forward, where you will be involved in real office firefighting engagements. By real, I do not mean literally fighting a fire, I am referring to getting involved in a crisis that needs to be addressed today, or it will have a damaging impact on the business, e.g. a product or service did not get to a VIP client as promised, essential stock has not been delivered, poor public reviews, an accident has occurred, a senior manager is upset with the service etc. There will be great concern around the implications of the crisis, it will be happening in the present moment, and you are reactively responding to it.

Initially, your goal is to put the fire out before looking for a longer term resolution. This second part of the process, which is looking for the longer term resolution, is often the piece of the process that is forgotten as another fire takes over your attention. Firefighting keeps your attention in the past and in the moment, rarely does it allow you the time to be proactively thinking and planning.

For some, working in a high-energy environment and having a continuous level of stress placed upon them works for them. 'The Energiser' (STEP© style category, source: The Bute Group) is at their happiest when they are active. They thrive on new and unknown tasks. Repetition does not work for them. They are typically high-energy individuals who enjoy being the centre of attention. They will take on new tasks with relish. They usually talk more than listen. These individuals love the excitement around firefighting. For others, it can be damaging to their wellbeing.

'The Thinker' finds comfort in working in a quieter environment with the time to think through the task at hand, or the question being asked, before any form of demonstrative action is required. Typically, 'the Thinker' does not like to be the centre of attention and prefers to take the 'back seat'. They are usually quiet and are good listeners.

Source: The Bute Group, Working Styles Evaluation.

Regardless of your style, persistent firefighting is not only damaging for you, it is also exhausting for your team and the business as a whole.

Be very careful of firefighting. It can easily become a habit, an addiction, the more you receive recognition for being a firefighter, the more you may strive to keep the adoration coming. Being known as someone others can rely on in a time of need creates spiralling behaviour, and before long the issues don't need to be of grave importance. You will be looking for issues to fix, and people will be coming to you with any issues, regardless of complexity. As you continue to fix other people's issues, they will pass small issues to you as your personal brand is the 'go-to person' and of course the giver of the issue will not want to spend their own valuable time on it when they can spend their time on the 'higher value' tickets that enhance their personal reputation and brand. Others' insignificant and small problems that you continue to fix will hinder you and your team's ability to carry out the work allocated to you and agreed by you.

SUPERHERO SYNDROME

Creating desperate situations that need fixing and being called upon to be the fixer creates a superhero syndrome, and your personal and social identity becomes part of this. You will relish the attention bestowed upon you, and you'll be looking to be reactive more so than proactive. The issue with being reactive is it never allows you time to step back and consider longer term fixes. For some firefighters, they don't want the drama to stop.

Your personal reputation and brand will suffer as a result of you only focusing on fixing. People will see you as the 'go-to' person for any issues. And whilst it's important to be seen as helpful, you don't need to be everyone's fixer. That mentality keeps you in the reactive mindset. If that is your primary mode of thought, consider the impact of this on the business plan. How do you drive your business and team forward when all your consideration, effort and energy is focusing on fixing the past?

I suspect you are thinking that it is important to stabilise and then build on your existing platform. This is absolutely correct; equally, knowing that everything doesn't have to be fixed, some processes, tasks and outcomes can fall by the wayside without any impact on the business. Your job as senior manager is to recognise which of those are the ones you can afford to let go. Whilst considering the solution to the existing issues, there is also the requirement to consider what the next stage would be, e.g. once you've fixed the supply chain issue, how do you improve upon it?

Remember, proactivity drives future issues and the company forward.

As you focus on being the superhero, it is very common for you to take on a martyr persona whilst secretly loving the attention. The issue with this is, and it's worth considering where you have observed others behave like this, what did you think of their behaviour? The superhero/martyr likes to tell everyone who will listen how others only ever come to you with issues, woe is me, and with an exasperated tone you say, "plenty of other people are capable of fixing it, why don't you go to them?" The truth being that if people started going to someone else, you would be greatly offended and annoyed, and when others offer to help, you refuse. You are after all the hero, the fixer.

DRAMA IS A TIME AND ENERGY STEALER

Whichever way you parcel this up, firefighting is a form of drama, and drama is a time and energy stealer. It takes a lot of energy to sustain the effort required to be the superhero. It can drain your day when your focus is on firefighting. It will drain your personal reputation and brand, and most often without you even realising it. Whilst initially the business will be appreciative of the help, that will only be sustainable if you are able to carry out your existing requirements in parallel to the firefighting. I have yet to observe anyone balancing both the job with their superhero ego successfully.

TIME TO TAKE THE CAPE OFF

Step back, take off the cape and know which fires you need to extinguish; your choices have a direct impact on you and your team. Which fires will directly impact you, which fires will indirectly impact you, and therefore you choose to support, and which fires have no impact on you, and therefore you direct the task to someone who is better qualified to resolve the issue?

You have a team, if the issue that needs to be corrected has direct impact, use your team and other resources. One of the greatest ways to show your trust in your team or a particular team member is to empower them to resolve an issue or issues. Give them the authority to make decisions and allow them to run with it; you are there as their support. You are not alone, do not get into the habit of seeing yourself as the lone superhero, and that you and you alone will only be able to resolve the issues. Focus on your role and your team's success.

PROACTIVE MANAGEMENT MUST OUTWEIGH THE REACTIVE

As a senior manager, you are caught between a rock and a hard place. Executive leadership focus is on strategic and proactive, whilst first-line managers are operational and reactive. And you are or will be the middle manager. Your responsibility (as you would have read earlier) is to ensure that your teams are operating and reacting to the business requirements and that the business requirements are challenging and yet realistic. In other words, you are the middleman.

How do you achieve that? You have a good sense of the ideal world versus the real world. The ideal world is the strategic plan, the business plan from the executive leadership team, and the real world is the productivity and output from your direct reports and extended team.

The reality is that you will always be striving for more. Senior managers, possibly more than any other role, are exposed to and driven by success. Their KPIs are results driven; their delivery is tangible.

APPLYING THE 80:20 RULE

In an ideal world, as a senior manager, you would spend 80% of your working week (four days) being proactive with 20% (one day) being reactive. The reality is, for most managers, that those statistics are inverted. However, if you make the time and the space to sit back and consider what proactive looks like versus what reactive is, you have a fighting chance of altering the ratio.

A great place to start with proactive management is dealing with the reactive issues and concerns. You may wish to start this by referring to or compiling an incident database. This will hold incidents that are relevant to your service or products and stand in the way of you reaching your goals as agreed through the business plan. Once you have that understanding, ask your direct reports to start reporting on these incidents and transfer the ongoing responsibility of these, trust the team to know and take ownership for the output.

Consider what are the recurring top three issues within the departments? Which top three incidents have the widest reach? Which top three incidents impact the VIPs? Which top three incidents impact your clients, both internal and external? The objective here is to gather a report that shows where your team is spending most of their time resolving recovering issues, and which can be dropped. Now you and your direct reports have that understanding, it is time to get to the root of the problem proactively. Are you the best person to do this? Is there someone in the team who is more experienced? Is there someone in the team who would benefit from being developed in this area?

Once the root cause has been identified, now you can devise a plan to resolve the issue permanently. Again, are you the best person to carry this out? Is there someone in your team who is better at this than you? Is there someone within the team who would benefit from the development in this area?

There is a real and urgent requirement to fully understand the essential areas within your business. If there was a service outage or other potentially business crippling occurrence resulting in the business being unable to deliver, the consequences of which would result in a detrimental impact on revenue, staff or environment, you need to be fully aware of these areas. Equally important is to understand those areas that are qualitative, that build the company's reputation and brand; these areas whilst not directly generating revenue will have a substantial indirect impact on revenue.

These points are often the areas that stand you apart from your competitors; they are those small acts that keep your customers coming back. They may include relationships, partnerships, sponsorships etc, they are relational rather than product or service related. Having a formal plan of how you would manage to continue with business as usual (or at least this being perceived by the outside world) is important. Know what the far-reaching implications are, what the fallout of these areas going wrong would be, and negate the risks by having a business plan that is tried and tested. You may recognise that these areas are often, although not limited to, your company's unique selling point (USP) and unique value point (UVP).

By utilising your team, again, you reinforce your trust, motivation and productivity. In addition to this, it frees your time up to be more strategic. As you support your team through identifying problems and solutions, you start to identify business improvements. Win:win.

CHAPTER REFLECTION AND ACTION PLAN

Helping others is a good thing; looking for issues to fix for others is not. Playing the superhero and wanting to solve everyone else's problem takes you away from what you are employed to do. Added to this, it places unnecessary stress on your team who will be vying for your time, or worse, left to carry out the fixes. Take off the cape and refocus your time and attention on where it is required.

CAMERON

Cameron likes to be helpful; she realised that actually a bit too helpful, maybe she did like wearing the cape. She could tie this back to the need to be liked and not to upset people. She also noted that this was not assertive behaviour, win:win. It may have initially felt like a win for her when she was helping others; however, this has now become a burden. It was definitely a win for the requestor as they could continue with their own role, and Cameron and her team would work vigorously at sourcing and providing a solution for the requestor. Following working through the exercise below, Cameron began to make changes.

She politely started by directing those issues that did not impact her or her team to the correct person. She knew she would have to do this every time a request came in; she not only had to change her behaviour, but she also had to stop others coming to her. She also authorised her direct reports to do the same, and she backed them every time.

She had her direct reports produce reports on 'exceptional' work they carried out, that is work outside of their remit.

In order to move away from the drama, she repositioned and reframed her team's outputs. She instructed that they set up an incident report and report on the top three issues. She worked with the team to research root causes and solutions. She set up recurring fortnightly meetings with her direct reports to review the report and discuss progress. She planned on handing over this initiative to her direct reports after she could see the process was working. She would also hand over the ownership, although she would continue to hold accountability for the progress.

She ringfenced recurring weekly time in her calendar to reflect on her progress and that of her team. In addition to this, she held structured monthly meetings with her manager to ensure that she was kept informed of the progress and updates, and to receive feedback on her own and her team's performance.

Cameron was really starting to feel like a senior manager and was receiving meaningful feedback that confirmed that others were also seeing her as a senior member of the company.

OVER TO YOU...

1. Prior to agreeing to 'fix' a colleague's issue, take time to stop and breathe and consider if it is your or your team's responsibility to resolve the issue.

   a. Is this your responsibility?

   b. Does the issue directly impact you?

   c. Indirectly impact you?

2. Is there someone else better suited to sourcing the solution from outside of your team?

3. If you agree to the fix, who will carry it out?

   a. How long will it take them?

   b. By saying yes to the fix, what are you saying no to?

   c. How does this enhance your team's (and therefore your) reputation and brand?

4. Construct an incident database which focuses your attention on your team's issues. You will refer to this in more detail later in the book.

CHAPTER 4

HARD FACT, YOU THE MANAGER ARE OFTEN THE CATALYST OF YOUR TEAM'S TROUBLES

85% of employees worldwide are not engaged or are actively disengaged in their job. (Gallup 2017)

The above statistic is a sobering thought. 85% of employees worldwide are **not** engaged or are actively disengaged in their job.

Let me share some further statistics. The Bute Group (2020), runs three ongoing surveys, they have hosted these surveys since 2017. The question recipients are asked: to the general workforce, if you had the option, would you re-employ your manager as your manager? As at July 2020, the response was 81% would not re-employ their manager.

This same question was posed to first-line managers: if you had the option, would you re-employ your manager as your manager? Eighty-eight percent responded that they would not re-employ their manager.

The question targeted at senior managers: if you had the opportunity on Monday to re-employ your existing direct reports or employ a new team of your choice, which would you choose? And the response was 79% responded that they would like to employ the team of their choice.

All of the above statistics in this chapter show that more people are not engaged than are within their role. What is also interesting is that employees are not happy with their managers, and managers are not happy with their teams. Go figure!

What is the issue? It is definitely more than just bad management; however, bad management plays an immense part in this. From empirical observation, it is clear that managers and leaders can turn a happy, confident individual into a stressed, underperforming and lacking individual. Whilst managers can also create a platform of harmony and productivity within toxic companies.

Whose responsibility is this to correct? The reality is the responsibility lies with you, the manager. An inexperienced manager will always look to blame external sources for issues around motivation and productivity, and that external source is often the team. I hope as you read this that you consider your team to be a valuable resource, and they do you.

YOUR TEAM RESPONDS LIKE FOR LIKE

There is typically one of three paths of engagement a new senior manager will take upon promotion. One, they will get overly involved with their direct reports team; two, maybe that they deal only with the direct reports with little or no engagement with the extended team; or three, they aim to balance their engagement.

Too involved

An inexperienced and non-confident manager will become overly involved with day-to-day operations. This will reduce your direct reports' perceived level of authority amongst their team, your peers and your senior leadership team. If this carries on for an extended period of time, it will be perceived that you, the manager, are unable to manage the promotion, or regret having taken on the promotion due to your inability to carry out the role. If this was an internal promotion, it will be important that you learn to delegate your previous responsibilities, and that you find your happy medium in terms of engagement, delegation and stepping back.

It is normal when starting a new job that you get to know your team well; however, once this has been established you must step back as it will appear that you don't trust your team to deliver. It also highlights a level of immaturity within your management experience. An experienced senior manager will know at what level they need to be involved. Their focus will be placed squarely on the proactive and strategic requirements of the executive leadership team and the reactive operational management of their direct reports.

Find the balance between being professionally friendly, micromanaging, and wanting to be best friends. If you feel that you need to get a deep understanding of the team to a micro level, a level of engagement and understanding that requires a deep dive, consider 'skip level 1:1s'. Skip level 1:1s allows you to hold structured meetings with your direct reports' direct reports, that is, your extended team. This can be a delicate process, as you certainly will not want the inference to be that you don't trust your direct reports. Therefore, gain buy-in from direct reports before carrying these out or before communicating your plans to the wider audience. Ensure that this session is seen as positive and not an opportunity for team members to use it as a session to whinge and moan. Have a clear agenda and idea of outcomes.

If your direct reports are worried about the feedback you may receive from their team, then first address these issues and concerns with your direct reports. If they persist, I suggest that you have a bigger issue here and may need to coach and mentor your direct reports. The objective of skip level 1:1s is that you have an opportunity to engage your extended team, you can develop your networking and gain a greater understanding of what is happening at ground level, whilst communicating your news and giving your team direct exposure to you, their senior manager.

Cutting all ties

Not acknowledging your extended team at all suggests a lack of caring. This again can be perceived as an inexperienced manager not having the time or recognising the importance to engage, be open and friendly. It is not unheard of for chief executives and senior leaders to floor walk to engage and connect with their staff at least once a week.

A workable balance is to have conversations with your extended team; however, ensure that the team go to their own manager in the first instance with their questions, queries and suggestions. And that you too utilise your direct reports to communicate to their team your instructions and wishes.

Your team will place value on your perceived level of trust

Your team place value on your perceived level of trust in them. If you are still holding on to your previous responsibilities due to lack of resources, it would be of great importance that you consider the required and existing resources to carry out your job effectively. Consider the monetary costs of you carrying out your previous responsibilities versus a more junior member who will be paid less than you. Consider the cost of you carrying out your previous responsibilities and the time taken away from carrying out your new role. What will be the cost of being reactive versus proactive?

It also suggests that you do not have the confidence to commit to the new role. Often you will have been promoted because of your existing performance within your previous role and that role and responsibility becomes a security blanket. It may boost your confidence as you know you can carry out your previous role well, after all, that is why you were promoted.

This behaviour can also be true when you have started with a new company. You look to replicate the success and comfort of your previous role by carrying out tasks that are familiar and easy within your new role. You may even create tasks that allow you to exhibit your competence in carrying out more junior tasks to demonstrate where your strengths lie. Be careful, what this exhibits is your lack of ability or initiative to step up into your new role.

Again, gain clarity around the new expectations of your role, look at the essential tasks that you are now to carry out and compare with your previous responsibilities. Ideally, if you've carried this out correctly you will see that very little if any of the actions need to be carried out by you. If it is the case that your confidence is not on a par with taking and committing to your new role, it is time to plan for the handover of your previous tasks and responsibilities to free up your time to continue to develop your strengths and transition your limitations into workable strengths.

Continuing to hold on to previous responsibilities after a promotion highlights several points. One of these may highlight you do not trust your new team to carry out your previous responsibilities. Ask yourself why you are not passing these on. Lack of trust? A comfort blanket for you? Not sure how to delegate effectively?

Delegation for managers often gets easier with seniority. If your delegation technique was not strong as a first-line manager, this is absolutely an area of management that you will look to strengthen.

If your new role is not fully formed and is currently light on responsibilities, refer back to your key roles and responsibilities, is there not enough in this to keep you busy? If the answer is you have spare time, consider where your time would be better spent, it certainly won't be in carrying out a more junior role. It is more realistic and likely you will not have the time to carry out your new role efficiently and effectively if you continue to carry out your old role. Consider, who in your team could benefit from taking on more responsibilities, who could you develop to carry out your previous tasks? Who would benefit from that level of trust and authority that this would establish?

I suspect that you may be seeing a requirement to continue with your previous responsibilities due to lack of resources to delegate to. This is particularly true when going through an internal promotion. There may be an expectation that you continue with your existing role and take on the new role. If that is the case, there is some work to be done to create space to carry out your new role.

At a later chapter in the book you will be tasked with an exercise to capture your existing resources, including capabilities. This exercise will give you a clearer picture of where you can start the delegation process, which resources are available, who has the abilities, who will have the capabilities through development and potentially who would like to take on your previous role. This may be a development, and promotional opportunity for an existing member of your team. What a great win for you and them (win:win) if you were to develop and promote someone into your previous role. This also highlights the level of trust that you have within your team. Individuals want and need to feel trusted to not only carry out their role but to also support their managers and colleagues.

It may be you actually don't trust your team to carry out the responsibilities; you may consider them inferior in terms of skill set, maybe their attitude isn't up to scratch, maybe their standards aren't the same as yours, or they won't do it the same way as you did it. For the most part, these are just excuses to hold on to a task that comforts and is reassuring. If it is true, compare existing abilities with required capabilities. A great move would be to engage HR and your manager and devise a development plan to empower your team to take on additional responsibilities. HR and your manager should recognise this as a positive intervention by you as a manager who is looking to develop their team, themselves and get the best ROI for the business.

A further KPI of a successful manager is the level of trust they place on their team. If you can trust your team, it is time to carry out an exploratory exercise that is based on facts and explores what your team is capable of carrying out. This exploratory exercise often leads to the manager noting that their perception of the team's capabilities was incorrect. It was their own bias against the team, and not the team's inability to carry out the work.

Word of caution: if you are taking on a team who you have no history with and are seeking others' feedback, remember that poor teams are generally the result of poor management and that people may be quick off the mark to blame the team when, in fact, it was the previous manager who didn't manage the team, task or expectations effectively.

The team is mirroring you

As you become more integrated within your role, you will find your style; ensure that this reflects your ideal personal reputation and brand as per your earlier exercise on page 32. If the team are simply not getting things right, stop and look at your communication style.

It is not the responsibility of the team to know your style and work accordingly; it is your responsibility as a manager, even more so as a senior manager that you recognise others' communication styles and act accordingly. If the team's behaviour and attitudes aren't as you wish, it is likely they are mirroring your behaviour. Or it is a hangover from their previous manager.

As you will recall from the KPIs of a great manager, one of the measurements is the team's knowledge of their existing goals and objectives, and how informed they are of the business and the bigger picture. Knowledge is empowering, not just to you as a senior manager, but also to your direct reports and your extended team, your peers and to your manager. Share the knowledge as this will translate into a team that has a greater understanding of the big picture and therefore, recognises the needs of the business and how they fit into their responsibilities.

The internal supply management chain is important to understand for you and the team. Allow the time to understand and recognise where the internal supply chain feeds into others and where and what the impact will be if your teams don't deliver. This increases confidence in individuals and confidence in others of you and your team's capability and understanding. What does that mean for you and your team's reputation and brand? Understanding and successfully delivering within the supply chain will enhance personal reputation and brand.

Be the role model, what would a productive and motivated team look like to you? Unpack the question, what does productive mean to you as a senior manager? Will it be either quantitative or qualitative results? Or both? Is it just outputs? Or should you include inputs? Should you be measuring engagement with clients? With team members? With others? What makes sense to you in your industry and company may not make sense to others, ensure you understand how these measurements fit back into your business plan, culture and values.

Be open with the team on what and why you are measuring and benchmarking. Ensure that you are demonstrating the culture, values and guiding principles that you wish to see and measure within your team. Food for thought, ask your team what they believe you, as their manager, should be measured on; it may be eye-opening.

Ensure both yourself and the team know the benefits and value of the outcomes. This will only happen when you know the big picture, knowing where the value is in your role, and your team's output is crucial to gather this source information from the team, your clients, your manager and others. Understand where the team is benefiting others as well as where the team are (hopefully unaware) hindering others. Creating a team that is both productive and efficient or creating a team that is unproductive and inefficient is a choice. It will take time; it is worth the investment. You will make mistakes on the way; you are human, learn from them and move on.

TAKE CARE OF YOUR TEAM AND THEY WILL TAKE CARE OF YOU

"To explore the challenge to the human soul in organizations is to build a bridge between the world of the personal, subjective, and even unconscious elements of individual experience and the world of organizations that demand rationality, efficiency, and personal sacrifice… we must be willing to shift our viewpoint back and forth between what organizations want of people and what constitutes human complexity: the contradictory nature of human needs, desires, and experience." (Briskin 1998) In other words, it is give and take. Know what you need to work towards and understand that those who carry it out, like you, are human. The complexities of personal life impact the contribution to work and vice versa; if home life is good, work typically is. When work is going well, it follows that home life generally will too. However, the opposite of this is also true. It is a unique person who can switch from work mode to personal mode without thinking about work in their personal time and again, vice versa.

CHAPTER REFLECTION AND ACTION PLAN

Ask yourself why you are reluctant to hand over or let go of your more junior tasks. This is not exclusive to senior managers; managers will respond that the team will not carry out the work to their standards, or as quickly, or in the same way, or, or, or. Have you considered that the team may carry out the task better than you?

CAMERON

Cameron recognised that at times she was short and snappy with her teams. She had a young family and was sleep deprived. She decided to share this with her teams. Their response was very supportive of Cameron as a mother and a manager. Cameron revealing this level of vulnerability created a shift in the team dynamics; it became more open, with the team discussions becoming less guarded.

She decided to use this opportunity to engage her direct reports further with her work, and she worked through the exercise below. What became apparent very quickly was her direct reports were open to learning and taking on additional responsibilities. Cameron discussed with her direct reports the law of balance and agreed through their 1:1s that she would support them on delegating some of their work to members of their teams, win:win.

OVER TO YOU...

1. Refer back to your exercise from 'Managing your working styles, responses and behaviours' and the list of recurring tasks.

2. Update the list if required.

3. Review the tasks and consider if they produce high-value outcomes to your role. Or are they low-value outcomes within your role? Be honest, if in doubt, engage your team.

4. List your low-value outcomes (and without labelling the tasks, low-value), engage your direct reports to create a handover plan.

CHAPTER 5

EMPLOYEE COACHING

Employee coaching is that one thing that a manager can do that moves them from being an **OK** manager to a great manager. When delivered authentically and honestly, employee coaching can be one of your best tools; the motivation that I've observed employees take away from coaching sessions has been incredible. The primary goal with coaching is to unlock the coachee's potential.

Let's clear up a couple of things first. The difference between a mentor, a coach and training.

MENTOR

A mentor is typically more senior than yourself and has greater experience. They will generally guide, direct and feed back scenarios and situations that they have found themselves alongside the solutions and outcomes.

A mentor tends to be specific on a subject, i.e. you may have a mentor who works with you on a change management programme, it will be similar to one that they have run in the past, and they will have extensive knowledge, thoughts and opinions that they are happy to share with you.

TRAINER

A trainer is often prescriptive in their delivery. They have an objective, you have an objective, and the trainer will deliver on this. A trainer often delivers in a group environment and focuses on the group experience.

COACH

What is a coach? A manager who is taking on the role of a coach will work with their coachee with both their mentor and trainer hat on. Added to this, they will empower the coachee to set goals, agree objectives and action plans. The coach is often perceived to be more empowering than either the mentor or the trainer as the coach designs the coaching sessions around the individual's requirements, not the situation, not the group.

The coaching relationship is focused on the coachee's growth, and the growth will often be tied into the bigger picture, i.e. the department and the business goals. The manager who is taking on the role of an internal coach carries out a different role from that of an external coach. Often with the manager/coach, the coaching topics are work-related. With an external coach, there is often a more holistic approach.

COACHING AN EMPLOYEE

When coaching a member of staff, there are two key areas to focus on: existing role and future career. Within the existing role, coaching often takes the shape of working with the coachee to enhance their skills. This involves being curious as to what the coachee believes can be improved for themselves, by themselves and sharing your observations and feedback. It includes considering developing the coachee into their next role; this may be an internal or external role.

Coaching employees on their future career aspirations again allows you to be curious to where the coachee sees their career unfolding. You, as their coach, support, make suggestions and share feedback.

The coach

You, as the coach, must keep in mind that you have a daytime job and not take on too much. When you enter into a coaching relationship with another, you have to be prepared to leave your day-to-day work issues, concerns and workloads at the door. Alongside this, leave your ego and your personal opinion regarding the coachee. Coaching is about productivity, not personality. It is important to set the tone and expectations of the coaching relationship, what can and cannot be discussed, what you as the coach will share with others, what is confidential, your expectations of the coachee, and what the coachee can expect from you as the coach.

A good coach will be curious about their coachee, and ask pertinent questions, and listen. Actively listen. There isn't a requirement as the coach to have the answers (this aligns more as a mentor's role), that's not your role; focus on what your coachee is saying, and then ask pertinent questions that expand on the topic, which challenges the coachee's current thinking and current exploration of the subject.

It is the coachee's responsibility to set the goals and objectives, including the action plan. Do not impose your opinion and thoughts on the coachee; it must be the coachee who makes the final decision on how they are going to progress themselves. It is your role to support and not to insist on it being your way (remember, leave your ego by the front door). That is not to say that you can't assist your coachee by potentially sponsoring their career aspirations and create opportunities for them to show their potential. Create a safe environment for your coachee to discuss issues, concerns and errors that they have made, knowing that you will not be gossiping or sharing that information with others. It is vitally important that you create an environment of trust and safety.

The coachee

The coachee within a coaching relationship is looking for advancement. That can be within their existing role, it can be topic specific, or it can be on career progression. The coachee is often looking for direction and advice. It is the coachee's responsibility to set the goals and objectives and take up accountability and ownership of the action plan. Whilst you're there to support, it's not your job to carry this out for them. Be clear around these expectations with the coachee and gain acceptance of this before commencing the sessions. The coachee brings the topic to the sessions; they are responsible for updates and sessions.

ADVANTAGES OF COACHING

There are a great deal of benefits to coaching your direct reports.

The coachee

The coachee will feel that the business and you are investing in their development, and for the most part, will reciprocate this through higher motivation and productivity levels. When the coachee owns their goals and action plan, which are often based around the company's requirements and availability, they will feel more motivated and thankful that the business is offering this opportunity. There is also the added bonus and benefits of the individual getting the undivided attention of you, their senior manager; this can be motivational. There will be an expectation that the coach will be able to advise or find out about the career progression within the business, support and advise the coachee on the best way forward. The coachee will also learn from the manager's inputs and suggestions.

The coach

The coach often feels like they are giving back and paying it forward. It is also a confidence and ego boost when you can share your experiences and wisdom and watch your coachee unlock their potential. The manager/coach will also benefit from a more motivated and productive team. It is a key component of coaching for the coachee to have set the goals and objectives, and that these are being results-driven; it develops an enhanced attitude for the individual focusing on what success looks and feels like for them.

The organisation

The organisation will reap the benefits of having more productive staff. Those employees will be driven by results and therefore motivated to reach them. The business will create and sustain a culture that is both caring and progressive. The company's reputation and brand will be enhanced by the quality of employees' delivery and outputs.

DISADVANTAGES OF COACHING

There may be some perceived disadvantages to coaching. One of these may be when you, as a manager, are coaching your own team members. The coachee may not feel comfortable sharing concerns, issues and errors they have made. This can often stunt the coaching relationship and inevitably leads to coaching been disbanded within the company. In addition to this, it is a commitment from both the coach and the coachee; businesses and managers may see this as a drain on resources and not a great return on investment. There will be times when the coachee isn't bothered about the coaching and does not see the value associated with it, and therefore puts no effort or return on the value of the coaching. This may be due to an inexperienced or disengaged coach who is not creating an environment that generates curiosity and engagement.

However, when conducted well and creating a coaching culture within the business, the advantages by far outweigh the disadvantages.

THE COACHING PROCESS

Chemistry meeting

It is worth considering the existing relationship between a coach and an assigned coachee. As an introduction, chemistry meetings should be held to ensure that the coach and the coachee are compatible and would like to work with each other. It is no slight on the coach or the coachee if either chooses not to work with the other. It is important to get a good match for the coaching to be productive and the relationship to blossom. This will inevitably unlock the coachee's potential and offer a greater return on investment for the business.

At the chemistry meeting, this is the ideal platform to share and discuss contracts, e.g. what can be discussed and not, length of sessions, frequency of sessions, expectations of both parties, cancellation periods etc. Confidentiality is particularly important to agree at the chemistry meeting so that both parties can decide whether it is a go or no go with the coaching relationship.

Coaching sessions

And the magic happens here.

There are several coaching methods that you may use; the **GROW** model is the most popular, this was created by the coaching legend John Whitmore in the late 80s. It is very simplistic in its approach. GROW represents Goal, Reality, Options and Will.

THE 'A' CLASS COACHING PROGRAMME©

Within our coaching practice, we created and work with 'The 'A' Class Coaching Programme'© (The 'A' Class Coaching Programme'© The Bute Group). The focus is on six key steps:

1. **Ambition** – What is the coachee's goal/aspiration?

2. **Assess** – Where does the coachee currently place themselves in relation to their goal?

3. **Arching** – How might the coachee bridge the gap between where the coachee would like to be (ambition), and where the coachee sees themselves (assessment)?

4. **Appraise** – As the sessions progress, is the coachee on track?

5. **Adjust** – How will the coachee accommodate the continuously changing environment?

6. **Applaud** – Celebrating the coachee's successes, and separately yours.

The reality of delivering coaching sessions is that you, as a coach, will not have to follow the order of the coaching framework. As a coach, you will work around the coachee's requirement, and that will involve using the steps in the order that makes sense at the time. It is necessary to apply all six steps by the end of the session.

1. Ambition – What is the coachee's goal/aspiration?

It is important to have both short-term and long-term goals set at the beginning of the coaching relationship. They must be meaningful and desirable enough to motivate the coachee to strive and want to meet them. The coachee's goals are not set in stone, and nor should they be, there must be flexibility around the ever-changing environment and client requirements.

For you, as the coach, it will work as a signpost in terms of monitoring your progress and session direction.

At the beginning of each session, clarify what the coachee would like from the session; session goals will assist you in keeping your coachee (and yourself) on track. It is also a good measurement of return on investment for the time and effort spent on the sessions, and, of course, is results-driven.

2. Assess – Where does the coachee currently place themselves in relation to their goal?

Your role here is to be curious around the coachee's perception of where they currently see themselves. Whilst you may be tempted to not agree, this is all about your coachee's perception. Ask questions, drill deeper. Ask for evidence-based examples; it is not unusual for a coachee to see themselves in a different place from where others view them. Asking for evidence-based examples allows you to challenge their assessment and reposition this where appropriate. You may also suggest the coachee sources feedback from others.

3. Arching – How to bridge the gap between where they would like to be (ambition) and where they are (assessment).

Now you and your coachee have a clear picture of where the coachee is, and what they are striving for, this part of the session is to review how they can bridge the gap. Two points to note: first, you may be looking at multiple goals here. You will have your big-picture goals (often set on the first session), and you will have the objectives that your coachee has brought to today's session. Second, the overarching goal will not be resolved in one session. If it is, you need to work with the coachee to create bigger goals that are more challenging and compelling to want and warrant change. Remember, coaching is about unlocking your coachee's potential.

4. Appraise – As the sessions progress, are they on track?

Time to check in on how the coachee perceives their progress. Please remember a fundamental goal of coaching sessions is to unlock the coachee's potential. For that to take place, progress must be happening. If your coachee is not progressing, the goal may not be motivational enough, it may not be their goal, or you may not have explored them and uncovered their true motivations they would want to work towards the goal. The goal should be inspiring enough for them to get up early and stay up late.

5. Adjust – Accommodate continuous change environment.

Whilst it's not unusual for the overarching goals to remain the same, the objectives will frequently require adjusting. With the focus being on the individual's current position and their clear progression, when business changes, new legislation is introduced, updated business plans are revealed, you and the coachee need to be aware of these changes and adjust their action plan and objectives accordingly. As a coach, encourage exploration of alternatives.

6. Applaud – Celebrating their successes and yours.

Congratulations, congratulations, congratulations and well done. Ensure that your coachee steps back and recognises their progress and their potential. This is a point of celebration, therefore celebrate.

For you personally, a senior manager who is carrying out a role as a coach, you have supported the coachee to get to a point where they have something to celebrate. Step back senior manager, see your input, and for you, celebrate your success.

Post session

It is important that the coachee feels that they can approach you through additional and agreed channels, e.g. email, phone or open-door policy during sessions. Check in on the coachee to strengthen the coaching relationship and to reinforce that you are there as a support. Again, please remember you have a day job.

Post session is the opportunity for your coachee to start to unlock and demonstrate their potential; after all, this is all about them. Don't be tempted to micromanage or correct their path if they go off track. Obviously, if they are endangering themselves or others, then it is your responsibility as a senior manager to intervene as early as possible to ensure the safety of the coachee and ensure there are no health and safety or operational issues. Otherwise, explore the issues and learnings on the follow-up sessions.

CHAPTER REFLECTION AND ACTION PLAN

Employee coaching can be perceived as either a fantastic or a time-wasting initiative. It is not an initiative to be taken lightly. However, when managed correctly it pays dividends to you as a manager, the business and your coachee who will be driven and motivated. Taking on a role as an internal coach is not 'managing' a team member, it is not directing them; coaching is allowing the individual to own their choices and accountability. Coaching allows your coachee to bring the topic to the table and not for you to use the platform to delegate or instruct. You as the coach, must listen and support, not tell and do.

CAMERON

Cameron is making great strides with her teams. She is taking the time to host weekly team meetings with her direct reports and is currently holding monthly 1:1s. In addition to this, she sourced a copy of the existing formal coaching initiative from HR.

Cameron recognised this was a time-consuming initiative, and that she was on a steep learning curve herself, so she decided to revisit this in nine months. In the meantime, she would start to apply the 'The 'A' Class Coaching Programme'© framework during the 1:1s and team meetings to practise using the model and look for and nurture her own natural delivery.

OVER TO YOU...

1. Find out if there is an existing coaching initiative within the business.

2. Source a copy of the policy and procedures.

3. Consider if you understand the business well enough to volunteer as a coach.

4. Consider if you have the available time.

5. Can you create an opportunity to trial the process during your 1:1s or team meetings?

6. Might you offer to coach another manager's team?

7. Might it be worth another manager coaching a member of your team?

8. Is there an opportunity for you to be the coachee in the process with someone from the leadership team as your coach?

CHAPTER 6

THE COMPANY'S STRATEGIC PLAN

And now to the business requirements. Business plans are not set in stone, and nor should they be, there must be flexibility around the ever changing environment and client requirements. However, as stated earlier, a key responsibility of a senior manager is to know and translate their company's strategic plan, which will be presented as a departmental plan.

The business plan is often a year's snapshot of initiatives and goals with further high-level detail on the following three to five years' strategic plan. Some companies will have a strategic plan for a longer period, very few will have one for less than three years, although it is not unknown for some companies to not have a business plan at all. The organisation size and complexity are often reflected in the strategic plan and, therefore, the business plan. If coming into this senior management role part-way through the year, one of the first tasks is to gain a copy of the company's long-term strategic plan and the current year's business plan.

An internal business plan will have two key responsibilities: the first to inform the reader of what the goals are and how the business plans to meet these, and secondly as a working document to determine how successful the plan is or is not. As a part-owner of the document, I would add a third responsibility, which is to review and modify the plan as and when required, comparing actual achievements versus forecasted and modifying where required to meet or exceed the company's goals. The business plan is your working document.

KNOW THE RESULTS

It is vitally important to your success, your personal reputation and brand, and therefore that of your teams, that you understand, acknowledge and work in collaboration with others, often as part of the senior management team, towards the business goals. These goals will be measured on both quantitative and qualitative results.

Questions that you will want to know the answer to are: What are the KPIs? Which am I responsible for? What is the executive team measuring my success on? What are the expectations on me and my teams that have not been included in the business plan? Having a clear business plan for each of your teams is crucial. This business plan is the roadmap for the foreseeable future. Create your own version that typically will be separate from the company's business plan. However, it must directly feed into and support the company's. Your business plan should contain a map to success, including KPIs by team and/ or department, overarching goals and how these will be met, and is detailed to individual, team development and departmental level.

Thorough business plans often include a company overview, product or service description, industry and marketplace analysis, marketing strategy, operations planning, product development, people development, financial planning, management and more, hence the need for collaboration.

ADOPTING AND ADAPTING THE EXISTING BUSINESS PLAN

The business plan will impact your department alongside the others; ensuring you are part of an SMT (senior management team) that is cohesive and collaborative will support your and their success.

Have a clear understanding of others' expectations of you and your team, confirm your level of authority in making decisions, where you may be allocated a responsibility, where you have little or no control of the outcome. Reframe others' expectations when you are heavily reliant on others (outside of your teams) for the outcome, do not set yourself, your teams or others up for failure.

You may recall from the introduction chapter that assertive management is having the confidence to say no so as not to set yourself up or let others down, and this ties into the win:win mindset.

To gain buy-in, ensure your direct reports are part of this journey. Collaborate with those in the know, your team members, they are the domain experts, they have greater experience in the day-to-day and operations and can support and inform the business plan. Individuals within the business who have been here for some time and know the expectations and understand your team's outcomes.

Knowing your available resources and capabilities is crucial; if you are new to the team, you will possibly not have an understanding or even exposure to this information at this point. Part of your takeaway from this analysis will be knowing what the gap is between existing abilities and required capabilities, clarity around budget requirements and budget availability. The authority through your knowledge to challenge and support the plan, assertive delivery with win:win mindset will serve you well.

Your business plan should clearly have clarity around the reality and capabilities, and the challenges that you and your team will face in meeting the goals. Where will the team require support and development? What will be the impact on team growth? There should be clarity around budget and resources, ideal world scenario, what is required to meet the goals? Followed by the reality, what do we have to meet goals? And then the plan shows the bridge between both. You may wish to think through the A class coaching process and be very curious around the outcomes of your business plan:

1. **Ambition** – What should be the goals/aspirations?)

2. **Assess** – Where does the team/department currently place themselves in relation to their goals?)

3. **Arching** – How might the team/department bridge the gap between where they would like to be (ambition) and where they currently see themselves (assessment)?

4. **Appraise** – As the sessions progress, is the team/department on track?

5. **Adjust** – How will the team/department accommodate the continuously changing environment?

6. **Applaud** – Celebrate the team/department successes.

Your business plan will take effort and time to compile. There will be a requirement to consider the risks involved in meeting your assigned goals, what barriers may stop you reaching them? Consider loss of resources? Consider budget cuts? Understand these vulnerabilities and design a plan that is implementation ready to negate those risks. Communicating this to your manager, the executive leadership team and your team is important, show your support or challenge of the company's business plan, carry this out with confidence and composure, without whinging or an overzealous display, show that you are on board and supportive of the company's success.

CHALLENGING THE PLAN

To challenge the business plan, consider what this means. To carry this out, ensure that you are not in an emotional state (you may wish to recall the emotional intelligence exercise of recognising your hot buttons). Compile a balanced and thought through report of your concerns and where applicable the resolutions, include the value and benefits of resolving these concerns. Ask your direct reports for their input on this.

Engage your manager in discussion to be delivered without any aggression; assertive delivery is calm and grounded. Be very clear on the difference between assertive delivery and whingeing. Tone and pitch are key, as is the body language. Whingers don't win wars; they damage reputations. Assertive delivery will gain a level of trust and respect from others, who will want to work with you as your personal reputation and brand will be seen as grounded and thought through. Be honest and open with your challenges and support, remembering to highlight the challenges with resolutions, and show support around the areas you are in agreement with. A balanced approach is required.

In it from the start

If you have the good fortune to be part of the strategic planning process, the insights gathered will be invaluable. Having exposure to the executive leadership team and being part of the engagement will give you insights into where the individuals within the executive leadership team align their loyalties, where they support and challenge the business plan, having an overview of their individual relationships within the work environment and so much more. Being invited to sit at the table is prime real estate to enhance your personal reputation and brand, this is giving you the authority to get involved, therefore share your thoughts and opinions assertively, and expand your network. Be prepared and do not waste the invitation.

Communicate in a mature and thought through manner that does not exclude passion and opinion. Be heard and judged for the right reasons.

As you go through the business plan or the process of building the business plan along with the executive leaders and your senior management team, two key questions to ask yourself are "does this motivate me?" and "will it motivate my team?"

Know your motivators, what is it that will get you fired up and want to meet and even exceed the business plan goals? If you're positively fired up, the likelihood is your team will follow. Referring back to chapter 2, know your personal reasons and how do the company's strategic and business goals support your motivation and vice versa.

Your team's motivation is vitally important

Gain a sense of what the motivators are that drive your team; it will require you to spend time with them and this can be a good thing, be sure to listen and acknowledge their input, remembering 1:1s and skip level 1:1s. You will be aiming to gain a sense of their historic performance, productivity, motivational levels, ask the team leaders and other senior managers of other teams and gain a sense of the role you have in shaping their ongoing reputation and brand.

Your objective is to understand what the business plan means to your team, what are the implications of this on your team's performance, will it motivate them or demotivate them? With your high levels of motivation, you will be able to sell the bigger picture with authentic enthusiasm and drive. If you are managing a large team, it will be difficult to gain everyone's buy-in, don't aim for that, go for a large majority win.

As you get to know your team, recognise who are the key players and influencers. Influencers may not be holding a formal position of authority, they may be an individual within the team or even external to the team who has a lot of influence over the team's attitude and behaviour. Your team may look to them for guidance and their thoughts on new initiatives and changes before deciding on where they themselves stand. Again, being authentic, honest and transparent with these individuals, look to gain their buy-in, they are your ideal ambassadors. Spend some time finding out what motivates those individuals, and if this motivation can be played into the plan (again authentically) bring them on board, it will make it easier to bring the others over and it will, of course, support you and the business in reaching your goals.

Know and communicate the big picture

How has the business plan been communicated in the past? What worked and what didn't? Be sure to ask the questions. The senior management team (SMT) should be a good place to start with the questions. As will your team meeting platforms, also harness the less formal occasions to ask your team how and what they thought of the roll-out of previous business plans. This is your opportunity to learn from these conversations.

Once you know what and how to communicate the bigger picture, go ahead and do it, do not over analyse, there will be the potential to get trapped within analysis paralysis, action is required, motion creates momentum. It is not unusual to assume others know what you know; they simply don't, they will not have attended the same meetings, put the same level of thought and work into understanding the business plan. Be explicit, clear and transparent with your message around the business plan, sell the plan, influence the team, create an energy around the delivery... bland, boring and vanilla messages never motivate and will only reap bland, boring and vanilla outcomes.

Drive home the importance of the business plan success for the individuals, team and business. Senior managers, in fact all managers, need to consider the individuals in the team when delivering a message and not make the message all about the business. If you get buy-in at an individual level, business success will follow. If your focus is purely on business success, the individuals will not feel part of the bigger picture or the goal, and therefore, won't necessarily buy in or deliver to the best of their ability. Business success often only plays a small part as a motivator in an individual's success, if at all. An individual's success within the business is a greater motivation; it is all about the individual's motivation.

If there is no business plan...

It's not unusual to work in a business that has no shared business plan. Typically, this tends to be smaller businesses or immature larger businesses. I have heard of businesses having business plans and not sharing them with the senior management team or the company as a whole. Go figure.

If there is no big-picture business plan to refer to, use this as an opportunity to collaborate with the senior management team, inviting the executive leadership team to consider devising one. If this is met with resistance, involve those who see the benefits and look to devise a plan that not only benefits you but also benefits the business. This process will compel you to explore and research the business in a more detailed approach. You will gather insights that would take months if not years to have gained exposure in alternative circumstances.

CHAPTER REFLECTION AND ACTION PLAN

Business plans always beg the questions: are there tangible KPIs? Is it clear where my contribution is required? How does my contribution fit into the bigger picture? Does this challenge and motivate me and the team to deliver?

There are, of course, many other questions that you would and should ask.

I have spoken with many senior managers around this subject of strategic and business plans. Typically, this is in a development environment. Concerns that have been highlighted frequently is that the leadership teams perceive the strategic and business plan exercise as a brainstorming session that results in a report, and then there's the sense that the job is done. Those who were in agreement with this felt the exercise was worthwhile; however, there was more that could be carried out to make the plan a living document. When it is perceived that the business is doing well, and often this means that the business is meeting their revenue and profits margins, the company continues as is and this is deemed acceptable; new initiatives will be put on the back burner as resources continue to focus on keeping the current trends of success on track.

The plan is not referred to on a frequent basis until there is a problem.

A second concern that is voiced is that senior managers are presented with a finalised document and are then expected to deliver without consultation. At this point the senior management team often go into overdrive with a reactive response of hurriedly translating the plan and this becomes fraught and at times unattainable.

Senior managers must be involved, and if not invited to the table find the confidence to ask to be involved early on in the process. In turn, you as a senior manager must bring in your direct reports to assist you in the translation, allowing them to bring their expertise to the table, get involved, share thoughts, expertise and opinion and of course buy-in and motivation for delivery. They will ideally in turn involve their team in garnering buy-in and motivation whilst sharing the big-picture thinking.

CAMERON

Cameron is new to company strategies and business plans. She had not received this exposure in her previous role. It felt like a big task; however, on reflection, it might just make her role easier. Knowing what the company wants, knowing her team and then bridging the gap would be a challenge. As she joined part-way through the year, she asked her manager for a copy of the strategic and business plan. She looked for her predecessor's plan, but there was not one. She carried out the exercises below and felt in a more ready place to step up to her role.

OVER TO YOU...

1. Ask your manager or a member of the senior leadership team for a copy of the strategic and business plan.

2. Unpack the plan, read through and highlight the areas that directly and indirectly impact you.

3. Compare actual delivery versus forecasted delivery as per the plan. This should give you an idea if you are on track, or not.

4. Devise an updated plan to meet the requirements; the business world is forever changing, the plan must be treated as an organic plan that changes with it.

5. Discuss with your direct reports and your manager and gain their input.

6. Propose your updated plan to the SMT, you will need and want their buy-in.

CHAPTER 7

DEVELOPING YOUR BUSINESS ACUMEN

WHAT IS BUSINESS ACUMEN?

Quite simply, it is understanding the business components that build success. The business components include finance, operations, competitors, marketing service, sales, HR etc. Business success for the business is a healthy and profitable business. Developing your business acumen will give you the confidence and knowledge to make informed decisions, challenges and educated guesses. It will also give you the confidence to engage with executive individuals. This will allow you to make educated and respectful challenges, propose relevant initiatives and be known for your depth of knowledge. Imagine what this will do to your personal reputation and brand.

A STARTER FOR FIVE

Understanding the external forces is important; exploring your market is a great place to start. Harvard Business School professor Michael Porter created the five forces, and it is now imaginatively called Porter's five forces. It is a framework used to assess the market environment; it explores how you're going to compete. It looks at market dynamics, substitute products, buyer and supplier power, and barriers to enter the market. Growth horizons are about how you're going to grow your business over time. Understanding this supports your input and challenges.

Working with the mindset that your teams and departments are a sub-business within the primary business is a good starting point. If you were to treat your direct reports and your responsibilities as if they were part of your own company, you would absolutely (I hope) put greater effort and energy into understanding your business. A great place to start with this is Porter's five forces. (Harvard Business Review 1996).

This framework looks at five key forces:

1. Competitive rivalry

2. New entrants

3. Substitution

4. Buyer power

5. Supplier power

Competitive rivalry

As a business, you will have competitors; you may even have internal competitors, other teams or departments that have a degree of crossover of services or products. Often you will class a competitor as a company of similar size, turnover, shares the same market, delivers similar offerings. Clearly, there are the obvious competitors; if you are in construction, they will be other construction companies: if you're in aviation, there are other airlines; if you are in leadership and management development, there are other training providers. These competitors will be the obvious ones to look at. How healthy are they as a business? What are their unique value points? What are their unique selling points and so forth?

Step back and consider who else are your competitors, not the obvious. Within construction, competitors may be a group of small construction companies who become a joint venture and tender for similar contracts. In aviation, trains would be a competitor as would video conferencing software, e.g. Microsoft Teams, Zoom and WebEx etc. In learning and development, e-learning would be a competitor, webinars, freelancers and more. As you start to understand your competition, you will start to gain a greater understanding of the company's or your department's strengths and limitations.

New entrants

Consider your business, how easy or difficult is it to get into the market? Within construction, I suspect it would be relatively easy, a van and tools will allow you to set up a small business, as it would within learning and development. However, aviation would be more difficult. To own an airline, you would be required to have the resources to purchase aeroplanes, hire qualified pilots and crew, licences to fly from particular airports etc. Within your industry, how easy would it be to set up a business? When it's simple you have a greater threat to your business, when it's more difficult there is a tendency to relax.

Substitution

Consider how easy it is for your clients to substitute your product or service. From an in-house perspective, consider how easy it is for the business to outsource your department or team. From an external perspective, how easy is it for your clients to provide your service themselves or go to a competitor? If you are in construction and offering a service to local councils to build and maintain public outdoor areas, how easy and cost-effective would it be for the councils to bring in an in-house team of gardeners and builders? If you are in aviation, how easy and cost-effective would it be for your clients to use Zoom instead of getting on a plane? If you're in learning and development, how easy and cost-effective would it be for the company to bring their offering in-house? Depending upon the niche, the uniqueness and complexity of your product or service will, in turn, dictate how simple or difficult it would be to substitute your product or service.

Buyer power

Customers are often looking for more from you for less money.

Consider how much power do your buyers have? Are you offering a unique product or is it widgets that may be purchased anywhere? Consider if you are supplying to internal customers, can they source the product elsewhere? Do not be complacent. Many years ago, I worked with a company who centralised their services within the UK. ICT, HR, finance, marketing and other departments were run from a central location with one central budget. This didn't work for the company as a whole, and therefore the CEO entrusted the individual departments to manage their own budgets. This worked so much better for them, particularly those departments which were geographically dispersed outside of the central location.

Then the complaints started; specifically, the ICT department was offering a less than acceptable service. The CEO had clearly heard too many times how some internal services were underperforming, and she informed all the departments that they could measure the internal services as if they were engaging with an external supplier, the premise being that if the 'customer' department could receive better services for the same cost or less, then they could use an external supplier. The CEO also informed ICT of this new change to process and procedure with the very clear message: improve your service or the service will be outsourced.

Nine months after the initial change to process and challenge to the ICT team, 40% of the overall ICT budget spend was being channelled externally. The impact on the internal ICT department was no improvement to the service, even though they were now servicing a smaller customer base.

Eighteen months after the initial change to the process and challenge to ICT, there was no internal ICT department. The service was being outsourced for a smaller budget and greater level of satisfaction. Some employees were TUPE'd over; the ICT manager was managed out of the role.

Supplier power

Suppliers are often looking for more money for less service.

Consider how much power do your suppliers have? And where does this power come from? Suppliers typically have power when they are in a niche market, and there are not many additional suppliers. Or suppliers get together and manipulate the markets.

As you consider buyer and supplier power, relationships can often play a bigger part than costs. That is, a buyer (client) will be more forgiving of a mess up when they have a good relationship with you, the supplier. They will also be prepared to pay extra, knowing that the relationship is solid, and you have their best intentions at heart. This is also true of suppliers. Treating a supplier/client relationship as a partnership rather than master/servant relationship should give you a greater return on your investment.

Using Porter's five forces will give you a greater insight into the business and your departments, this will also give you a greater understanding of the industry and business terminology.

EVALUATE TRENDS

To keep on top of your game, understand the trends that are happening within the industry, as this may potentially allow you and your company to become market leaders and to set new trends. View trends from many perspectives, what's happening within your client's industry? What technical changes are happening within yours? Who are the big players in the industry? What are they offering that is different and comparable to your offering?

KNOW WHERE RESEARCH AND DEVELOPMENT ARE GOING

Understanding where your industry is placing its importance in terms of research and development will be important in assisting you in determining where to focus your attention. Having a greater understanding of where your competitors are researching and developing will be of equal importance. Research and development are fundamental to staying ahead of the game. As a senior manager, it is vital that you are knowledgeable at both a business and departmental level. Senior managers are often perceived as the 'experts' by their direct reports and their own manager.

A healthy business is one that is striving to fulfil its customer needs, even before the customer knows or acknowledges those needs. Research will allow you to understand your clients' needs before they do and fill the voids before your competitors do. This is also true of your internal clients; finance departments would be expected to know of new legislation that impacts on the business, and the required process and procedures to deliver on it both within finance and their internal and external clients. Presenting a change plan to your clients will take away the mystery and stress. However, if your clients have to come to you with legislation that is related to your area, you will look incompetent, and your clients, the leadership team and your direct reports will lose trust in you. Think about the impact of that on your personal reputation and brand.

Within business acumen is commercial awareness; commercial awareness typically involves understanding the company, what are the company's success factors in both revenue and expenditure, understanding the industry enough for you to introduce initiatives that increase the effectiveness and profitability, in other words creating a high-performance culture. Part of this is the understanding and knowledge of the key financial drivers. Knowing the internal drivers and your external client's drivers is important and looking for initiatives or cutbacks that are cost-effective. This may feel uncomfortable and even a little scary; however, consider the risks of not being aware, of not knowing what is happening internally.

Experienced senior managers understand that there is a level of calculated risks that you will need to introduce in order to achieve both the business goals and your own. There are external factors that I urge you to consider and carry out an analysis. There is a well-worn framework to assist you in potentially carrying out this analysis and this is one of the best (at least in my experience), STEEPLE analysis of **S**ocial, **T**echnological, **E**conomic,

Environmental, Political, Legal and Ethical factors; what trends are appearing in the industry and sector? How relevant are they to the business? Can they be harnessed to increase revenue? What would be the value and benefits of the revenue generated versus the expenditure?

Taking time to research the above model or similar will give you greater confidence and your delivery of proposals will be in a confident, clear manner evidenced with good research and figures. When you consider evidencing your high-performance culture, consider the strategic and business plan, what is the duration of the strategic plan, 3 - 5+ years? Your high-performance culture should look to mirror the duration and beyond. High-performance culture is centred around sustainability.

Your company may present the above and more as part of their business plan; you may only need to carry this out at a departmental level. Be in the know, be the senior manager with the great insights, what a boost to your personal reputation and brand.

CHAPTER REFLECTION AND ACTION PLAN

Developing your business acumen will support your understanding of the strategic and business plan. It will allow you to unpack the detail further and carry out your own level of research for your departments. It will allow you to hold your own in discussions and even lead in places. This skill will enhance your personal reputation and brand. Developing your business acumen is an ongoing project, business changes, industry standards come and go, and competitors will always be there.

CAMERON

Cameron knew this was a weak area; she had struggled to fully understand the reasoning behind some of the business strategy. She recognised that to be taken seriously within her role and take her place at the table she needed to educate herself. As always, she worked through the exercises below.

Cameron decided the two key areas she would initially focus on were client and competitors. She started off by applying Porter's five forces framework, this gave her a greater understanding of the bigger picture. She had not completely appreciated how saturated the market was with competitors. This also gave her a greater understanding of the need for her company to stand out from the crowd. She got a thrill from this as her departments had a direct impact on this. She immediately arranged a meeting with the marketing manager to discuss this and get a greater sense of where the business was marketing itself. She then decided to carry out a STEEPLE analysis, first on the industry and then on the company's top five clients, which was an eye-opener. She had not realised the amount of technology out there that could potentially replace some of her department's services. Some work was needed.

OVER TO YOU...

1. Time to gain a greater understanding of the business – apply Porter's five forces.

2. From the competitors, who are your immediate threats?

3. Just how much power do your internal and external clients have over the service you provide?

4. What is the key area you must investigate in more detail?

5. Apply the STEEPLE framework.

6. Who has to be aware of your findings?

7. How will you engage the people who need to know?

You may not find anything new that you would want to share from your research; what you will gain is a greater understanding of what is happening within the industry and the company and apply this to future decisions and projects. Win:win.

CHAPTER 8

CREATING A HIGH-PERFORMANCE CULTURE

The culture within the business dictates the attitude and behaviour of its employees. Culture is driven by the strategic and business plan. If the overriding plan is to aggressively grow the business over a period of years, that, in turn, creates a culture that aggressively delivers. If the strategic and business plan is to grow the business ethically while harnessing the company values, then the employees will deliver within those parameters.

A business is focused on the bottom line, revenue and profits; this is not a bad thing – after all, businesses need to be healthy both financially and ethically to survive. Whilst toxic cultures within the business focus on bottom line, revenue and profits, this is often their only focus, how do we get the money and how do we keep it? They will encourage aggressive competition amongst their employees, promoting those who get the best results, regardless of the process. These companies often tolerate underperformance and use statements like, "it's better to have someone carry out a bad job than no one at all", "it's better to have a bottom on the seat, otherwise we lose the headcount." This scenario is due to the high turnover of staff and high levels of absenteeism and sickness. Who wants to work in that toxic environment?

A culture that promotes ethical and high moral standards and behaviours can still actively encourage competition amongst its employees, promoting healthy competition amongst their sales teams; this culture often motivates their employees to go above and beyond. A company that is promoting ethical and fair behaviour will not tolerate underperforming employees, negative gossip, office politics. This toxic behaviour is seen as unethical and unfair and will often be neutralised through positive intervention. Who would like to work in this environment?

Which of the two cultures above promotes and nurtures a high-performance culture? Which one will carry this out successfully?

Cultures, regardless of the sector, industry or company, are constructed of several elements.

THE CULTURAL WEB

Johnson et al. (2005) The cultural web provides a framework that identifies a number of elements within the organisation's culture. At the heart of this is the '**paradigm**', this represents what the company does, its mission, including its values. Six other elements support the paradigm.

Stories

There are the stories that circulate around the organisation with regards to the business. The stories are often heroic in their nature, how the business was built from the ground up, how a particular individual completed a feat of such great magnitude that everyone is in awe of them and the outstanding impact on the business. How a client was taken down a peg or two, how someone stood up at a meeting and challenged the senior leadership in front of the whole company and the company changed as a result. Over time the stories often become more and more embellished. The stories create and normalise circumstances that inspire employees to behave similarly, although very often in a lesser heroic fashion.

Symbols

Symbols are everywhere both inside organisations and outside. Logos, office location, allocated parking spaces and private office sizes for managers, quality of the office furnishing, space or lack of, company cars, company vans. Symbols create a sense of status and pleasure or pain; working in a luxury office block versus a rundown office building will help to attract and determine the motivations of individuals.

These symbols help shape behaviours; if the symbols are modern, fresh and clean, this often encourages similar behaviour. If the office is dilapidated, often so is the behaviour of the employees.

Power structures

Power structures are the individuals within the organisation that have impact on decisions, and the power can be based on personal influence, hierarchical positions, expertise etc. How these power structures are perceived, e.g. approachable, flexible, closed, elite etc. plays a large part in creating and sustaining the culture. If this works for the company, then sustainability is the goal; however, some power structures within companies can be perceived as toxic. This may be the behaviour within a service-providing department, a senior member of the company or even more junior individuals who may be perceived as influencers.

Organisational structures

Organisational structures, the structural hierarchies within the organisation, typically have different ways of interacting with other people. The flat hierarchies power structures will be quite different from those that have several structured hierarchies. Often the flatter the structure, the easier communications and controls are to understand.

Control systems

The processes and procedures that the organisation has in place to monitor what is going on. The levels of authority to carry out a role without the need to ask permission. There is typically more authority granted in a flat hierarchical structure. Where several layers of management are in place, the more diluted the authority to make decisions. Controls are in place to manage; however, when the controls are perceived as being too constraining, this can embed a sense of 'big brother' is watching and micromanaging.

Rituals and routines

These are the habitual activities, e.g. meetings, board reports, town hall engagements, emails from the chief exec, team meetings, 1:1s, even Friday afternoon rituals are often necessary to run the organisation, and can on occasions be considered more habitual than required. Consider the number of meetings you attend, was the time away from your desk worth your level of input or output received?

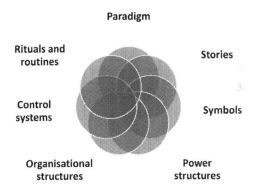

Adapted from Johnson et al. (2005)

Cultures may include these elements and more, and you may recognise some and have no awareness of other elements. Whilst the organisation will have a driving culture, a one size fits all often doesn't meet every individual's and every department's requirement. As a senior manager, understanding and recognising what works for your departments is vital. Making the necessary micro changes will be necessary and may take some time to embed. Knowing this and understanding how these changes will fit into the bigger picture is a necessary exercise. It is with a win:win mindset to enhance and be seen to improve morale and productivity.

What can you do to improve trust amongst your team? Alter your control systems?

As a senior manager, you will want to take the positive elements from your organisation and add to these to create your own high-performance culture within your department. This chapter's focus is on creating a high-performance culture. In order to take on new initiatives, roles and develop your team, there will be a requirement to carry out more. High-performance culture is a team effort. As a senior manager, this is not a demand and control movement; you don't demand a culture happens and then look to control it. You influence and get buy-in from those who will be impacted by it. High-performance cultures require vision, time, a team to implement and a great leader to support for long-term sustainability.

What are your visions for your departments? What visions does your team require? Which cultural changes can you manage or control?

RESULTS DRIVEN

Having a results-driven mindset is key to your success, as the old saying goes 'if you can't measure it don't report on it'. This is true most times; however, culture creates attitudes, and attitudes in themselves cannot be measured as behaviour is driven by attitude. You cannot gauge how productive or not someone's attitude is. If as a senior manager it feels (yes feels, you can see attitude in others' body language) if this is working for the department and is returning tangible results, then it is good to understand what is working for the team and replicate it. However, if the team and its individuals' attitudes are not appropriate and not working, then this needs to be rectified. And when change is required, measurements must be adhered to.

Consider which changes you can personally make, lead by example and demonstrate the attitude and behaviour that you are looking to create within the department; this will require you behave thoughtfully and respectfully, remember your personal reputation and brand. Often, when working with coaching clients they believe that they are demonstrating the correct behaviours; nevertheless, when this is observed or reflected upon, their unconscious attitudes, biases and behaviours come out to play and this can on occasions be detrimental to the overarching goal.

This can be observed more when the individual that is you, the senior manager, hasn't consciously thought through the behaviours that they would like to observe in their teams or wish to roll out across the teams. This again is based on having clarity around the stories (culture) that support the required culture that you are prepared to keep, the rituals and routines that you will introduce and/or remove, the control systems that you would like in place, the power structure of who has decided who manages whom or possibly the introduction of a flatter structure, the symbols that you have around the departments, e.g. individuals allowed family photographs and personal items on their desk, or is it hot-desking where a clean desk policy is mandatory?

The company culture will highlight the company's true values. It will be obvious if the company is living by the values that it promotes. Does the business follow through with its promises? Companies often carry out in-house surveys with the intention of communicating the results, does the company follow through with this? Executive leaders at their town hall meetings may 'scene set' by talking about future initiatives, do they follow through with update reports? Senior managers will communicate their future plans, do they translate this in a meaningful language that their own teams can get on board with? Or is it all about their own and/or just the business's requirements?

True company culture and values are highlighted when the business is under duress, observe what attitudes and behaviours are demonstrated, tolerated and even encouraged. To create a sustainable high-performance culture, it is important to have clarity around the existing culture, values and company principles. As a senior manager, having exposure to an honest view of this will allow you to create an environment where you are addressing existing issues and creating workable solutions within a culture that you are proud to be part of.

PERFORMANCE MANAGEMENT IS BUOYED BY MOTIVATION

It is not unheard of for a manager to respond to the questions "You're looking to create a high-performance culture? What are you benchmarking the existing performance against? And what does high-performance equal?" with "I don't know, I just need the team working harder."

You will hopefully have realised that in order to measure success, there needs to be both quantifiable and qualitative reporting. The first place to start is to benchmark your current performance management KPIs. Consider; how quickly are your operational tasks being turned around? How often are deadlines missed? How much time in advance of the deadline is the service or product being delivered? What are the current strengths within the team? What are the current abilities? What hidden strengths and capabilities are not being utilised? What limitations are there amongst the team? What limitations are there amongst the processes and procedures?

When conducting an exercise such as this, it is important to be transparent with your team with this type of initiative; be open around the goals and reassure the team that this is not a head-cutting exercise. Always engage the team for buy-in and ask them what they believe the answers are to the above.

If appropriate, ask your clients, both internal and external, for their input. Ask your peers within the senior management team as well as executive leadership team.

Gain a clear understanding of existing standards. Be ready and open to constructive feedback. Do not get offended, take it as professional and not personal. Look for trends and patterns in the feedback which will help you prioritise development plans.

Once this has been gathered, consider what you, in consultation with your teams, would see as a 'high-performance culture', how could and would you want to measure and report on it? Who will be privy to this information, and how would this new and improved high-performance culture impact others within the business? Which department or teams supply you with work and are therefore before you within the internal supply chain? How would your potential change impact these departments and teams? Which departments or teams do you provide a service to within the supply chain? How would your increased productivity impact those departments or teams? What and who else needs to be considered? As you consider this, think through who could put a spanner in the works of you successfully launching your new initiatives? Those individuals must be engaged as part of the process to gain buy-in to your initiatives.

Next, consider the resources available to increase performance; this isn't just a case of changing behaviours to increase productivity, you must also consider the emotional buy-in from the team. If you focus purely on behavioural change alone, the team will revert to type quickly. If you include attitude and mindset change and get genuine buy-in from the team, this sense of a high-performance outcome will become a longer term, sustainable initiative. Be honest around what would be required to meet the new high-performance culture, do you have buy-in, do you have the budget, do you have additional resources? Are the changes required realistic? Do not set yourself or your team up for failure. Consider the risks as well as solutions, values and benefits. You may also wish to have a plan B.

There are many questions to this stage, and the above is not an exhaustive list. What should become apparent is an initiative such as instilling a high-performance culture requires careful consideration and communication. It is not an initiative to take lightly. Or start and not complete because it is too hard or time-consuming. When conducted well, and by using the questions above as a jumping off point, you will evidence your final decision of go or no go.

TRANSPARENCY AND COMMUNICATION

Team meetings are a great platform to communicate big-picture thinking and gain buy-in. Once you have carried out some preliminary work, it is time to be open with your initiative. Gather the teams together and harness their expertise and knowledge, begin to gain a sense of where you are and what the new high-performance culture looks like. Bring the team along with you, gain an understanding of who the key players are within the team; this is often not the managers, this is those who have a greater influence on the team's responses and behaviours and look to gather their buy-in. Task other individuals to gather the evidence to prove or disprove current understanding.

Fundamental thinking around this is to know what great communication and content will look like. If your communication focuses on what's in it for the business, what's in it for you and what's in it for the team, buy-in is less likely at an individual level. Understand the impact of your communication and recognise and acknowledge why the individuals within the team would want to sign up for this, why would they want to work harder, smarter and so forth. Of course, you need to be clear on what the wins would be for the department, yourself and the business; it is just as important to also know what it is for the individuals.

BE PREPARED TO INVEST IN DEVELOPMENT

Jim Clifton states in the Gallup report 'The World's Broken Workplace' that "Only 15% of the world's one billion full-time workers are engaged at work." Clifton (2017). What does this mean when creating a high-performance culture? After all, productivity happens through engagement. Engagement involves communication, not just with your direct teams, but also with external divisions including HR and the senior leadership.

You're looking for the team to be upping the game. What investment will be required to meet the new challenge?

Be prepared to invest in the team's development growth. This is a motivational tool, most (not all) employees will appreciate and be thankful for the development. Point to note: telling your team you are investing in them, handing them a book, or giving them access to e-learning and telling them to complete this in their own time is not a winner. Consider other options if budget is scarce.

Is there an opportunity for your team to shadow others, be assigned an in-house mentor, can you assign time away from the desk to complete online learning during working hours? You may have to use your imagination… what's in it for the individual? On occasions, the reality is there are times when there is nothing in it for the individual, and that is fine, everyone needs to recognise and accept this. This, however, should be the exception and not the normal. Remember that individuals get paid to work; however, it is good leadership and management that motivates them to work more effectively and efficiently.

Short-sighted managers may respond with, "If I train them and they leave it will be a waste of budget and effort." Whereas a grounded senior manager should be thinking what does it mean if I don't train them? What will be the cost to the initiative? To the team? The business?

If I don't develop the team and they are unable to carry out their existing or new responsibilities (after all, a high-performance culture is about future-proofing the company's business health) how will this impact my personal reputation and brand?"

You, your direct reports, your line manager are all vital components in working towards a high-performance culture, not as vital though as those who will be carrying out the operational work. Those team members are the ones who should receive the recognition and support. They are the ones who should be front and centre of the praise. Their great or poor work greatly impacts your reputation and brand and that of your managers and the business.

CHAPTER REFLECTION AND ACTION PLAN

Culture is a key driver within business success or failure. From day one of walking into the business, you will have been exposed to the business culture. There are, on many occasions, differences between the culture that a business believes it portrays and what is actually being portrayed. This can be observed from the business induction through to the business exit interviews, and everything in between. As the senior manager begins to understand the real culture, and that it is layered, and heavily influenced by the managers' behaviour and therefore your behaviour and attitude will have a major impact on the department and company culture.

You often hear the culture when talking with clients and listening to the company's story around the clients. When your team members are talking about clients and colleagues, are the stories respectful? Do the stories create a sense of pride? Do they inspire the individuals to be better at what they are doing and offer a greater service or product? Or are the stories toxic? How do the organisation and department deal with mistakes? Is it a blame culture or support culture? Do teams and departments reach out to each other in stressful times and offer help, or do they actively sit back and watch it all implode, or will they actively and wilfully sabotage another department's success?

CAMERON

With Cameron's enhanced business acumen and greater understanding of the business, there was clear evidence for the need for her departments to be more productive. It was important to understand what that looked like. Cameron's first point was to consciously note what the current culture looked and felt like, and then how this would facilitate the changes required, or not.

OVER TO YOU...

1. Without judgment, start to note down the supporting factors that create your company's culture. Stories, symbols, power structure, organisational structure, control systems, rituals and routines.

2. Which of these work for your team and goals?

3. Which of these do you support?

4. At the very least, what changes need to happen to make your team's culture more engaging and productive?

CHAPTER 9

CONTINUOUS BUSINESS IMPROVEMENT

Stepping back and looking at the business and your department's requirements to meet the strategic and business plan is vital; knowing where your business and departments are at in terms of profit generation, and bridging any gaps is a must.

Simplifying the improvements within the business can come under two categories: the first, product/service and second the employees who carry it out.

There are many models out there for business improvements, Six Sigma, Kaizen, Scrum and more. All processes lead to one goal, to improve business health which is ultimately measured through the bottom line. Within business, staff wellbeing with a big push on mental wellbeing, healthy staff drive motivation and productivity.

Part of the measures on employee wellbeing is the volume of unauthorised absenteeism, timekeeping, staff turnover and productivity.

As I listen to others and observe people in the workplace, it seems that people are working hard to meet business goals, legislation requirements, client expectations and more. It can feel like a merry go round, going round in circles always looking to catch up with yourself. Give staff permission to own their choices. Trust them as the domain experts to know what is required and support them in achieving this.

FOCUS ON IMPROVEMENTS

The 80/20 rule, also known as the Pareto Principle, asserts that 80% of outcome is based on 20% of input. Eighty per cent of problems stem from 20% of your employees. Eighty per cent of revenue is generated by 20% of your clients. This would suggest that if you find the sweet spot, you will only have to work one day a week. The reality is that this is not the case.

Being the ideal manager working in the ideal company and the ideal environment would result in working 80% of the time in proactive mode and 20% in reactive mode. This is not an ideal world, and you will have to gauge where your time is best spent. First-line managers typically work to the opposite of this, 80% reactive and 20%; proactive and senior managers 60/40 or 70/30 in favour of reactive management. Continuous business improvements are both reactive and proactive. Get your house in order by eliminating the issues that steal your time now (reactive), and this should free up your time to be more proactive. Of course, an ideal world would be that you eliminate all reactive issues; the reality is it does not often if ever work that way.

SELL YOUR INITIATIVES

Continuous business improvement involves looking at and streamlining processes, and productivity will aid being creative and innovative when introducing the new ideas and initiatives. The business objective is to make the service or product as cost-effective as possible without cutting quality. This often strikes fear into new senior managers; it is immediately associated with redundancies and headcount loss. This does not have to be the case; by streamlining processes and having a clear plan of future initiatives, with those future initiatives highlighting benefit and value to the business, the redundant time for your team can be redirected to business improvements. Utilise your resources.

You will require a motivated team to buy into your initiatives and continuous business improvements. Remember, as you sell the initiatives to the team, you focus on what is in it for the individuals and the team. Immature managers tend to focus their conversation on one style, one audience and one outcome. Experienced and mature managers will recognise that individuals are just that, individuals. What will motivate one member of your team may not motivate another. What inspires one team, may not inspire your other teams. Your business pitch to the senior leadership team will be somewhat different from your business pitch to your own direct reports.

Consider who your audience is, senior leadership will have a greater investment in the business in terms of financial revenue compared to your direct reports. Therefore, senior leaders will want to know the numbers, the reports you are proposing, why and how it benefits the business, and this is best presented in monetary values. Whereas, your direct team will not be impacted directly by the monetary value, however, the impact for them may be the additional development, exposure to senior members, networking, career progression etc.

Of course, think about the order of communication. Understand what and when you can share your initiatives. Is it better to get the OK from senior management with regards to your proposed initiatives before you engage your team? Is it better to engage your team in order to be open and transparent before you engage senior leadership? Do they run in parallel? Only you will know the answer to this. Every company is unique, as are the individuals within the organisation.

YOUR STAFF ARE KEY PLAYERS IN YOUR INITIATIVES

Whilst your business improvement initiatives may include teams outside of your direct management, the majority of the operations with the new initiatives will typically fall within your own team's remit. Recognise the inputs and outputs of your team members.

Predictably Irrational: The Hidden Forces that Shape Our Decisions by Ariely (2009) has a chapter on 'The Cost of Social Norms Why We Are Happy to Do Things, but Not When We Are Paid to Do Them'.

"As Margaret Clark, Judson Mills, and Alan Fiske suggested a long time ago, we live simultaneously in two different worlds – one where social norms prevail, and the other where market norms make the roles. The social norms include the friendly requests that people make of one another. Could you help me move this couch? Could you help me change this tyre? Social norms are wrapped up in our social nature and our need for community. They are usually warm and fuzzy. Instant paybacks are not required: you may help move your neighbour's couch, but this doesn't mean she has to come right over and move yours. It's like opening a door for someone: it provides pleasure for both of you, and reciprocity is not immediately required.

The second world, the one governed by market norms, is very different. There's nothing warm and fuzzy about it. The exchanges are sharp-edged: wages, prices, rents, interest, and costs-and-benefits. Such market relationships are not necessarily evil or mean – in fact, they also include self-reliance, inventiveness, and individualism – but they do imply comparable benefits and prompt payments. When you are in the domain of market norms, you get what you pay for – that's just the way it is. When we keep social norms and market norms on their separate paths, life hums along pretty well…"

What is the significance of this? It appears to be true also in the workplace, where there are market norms, you get paid for the job; social norms also come into play. Consider within social norms being wrapped up in our social nature and our need for community; the community is the team and department. When a colleague asks another for some help, it is not followed up with "and I will pay you £££." No, the colleague if they feel part of the community will often assist without any want for payback.

How do you, as a senior manager, harness the power of social norms? The very first thing is to be honest and authentic. Do not see this concept as a tool to manipulate your team into delivering free work; you will find very quickly that your personal reputation and brand is damaged, and will be seen as a very poor manager.

Social norms tend to be relational rather than transactional, transactional being market norms. Social norms are not just favours; after all, as a senior manager, you don't want to be selling initiatives where the foundations are built purely on favours. Whilst there is nothing wrong with asking for a favour, you are a senior manager and with that initiatives must be built on solid goals, objectives and commitment.

So how do social norms work? First and foremost, they are delivered in an authentic and friendly manner. Social norms do not offer tangible rewards, which is if you do this, you will be rewarded with over time. It is asking the question of the team member who is carrying out the task, "What do you believe you will gain from this?" "What does this mean for you?" "How does this work for you?" You are not promising anything in return. This only works when your team member feels part of the team and the bigger community, that is their company. This only works if the team member has a sense of loyalty and liking for you. If you choose to ignore your team for the most part and then only engage with them when you want something, you will have to instigate market norms for any work to be carried out. This is a costly transactional relationship that results in a lack of loyalty and is managed through a master and servant relationship.

MAKE INITIATIVES CHALLENGING AND INTERESTING

Where possible, look to make the proactive initiatives challenging and interesting. Whilst the reactive initiatives will be around plugging the hole, the proactive initiatives should be bringing something new to the team and the department. Team members will often work on a more challenging task, mainly because they find it more interesting than the run-of-the-mill and recurring tasks.

As you consider continuous business improvements, there are several components that you should include in your consideration: impact, recurrence, value, benefits and cost.

Impact

Be results-driven in all improvements. In order to understand what to measure those results on, there is a requirement to capture the current impact of not introducing any new improvements. Who is impacted by the issues? How many people are highlighting the issue?

What would be the impact if you took no action?

When working in a proactive mode, consider the impact of leaving as is. What will be the impact if you introduce a new improvement? What is revenue versus expenditure, or value and benefits versus expenditure?

Recurrence

How frequently is the issue or concern occurring? If you are working in proactive mode, what would be the recovery use of the new improvement? Would the initiative be a one and done? Will it be used frequently?

Value

What value or expenditure is there currently in taking no action? What additional value will your improvement bring to the users and the business? Value can be measured in terms of monetary, reduced reliance on others, increased productivity, etc, quantitative amounts.

Benefits

What are the benefits of introducing a new improvement? Who would benefit from the improvement? Are they benefits that will be used, or bells and whistles that will help raise the value and revenue generated from the improvement?

Cost

What is the cost of doing nothing? What will be the cost of the improvements? What will be the return on investment?

Keeping the above in mind, it will be a real rookie mistake to have spent time, effort and communicated your proposed initiatives, including value benefits, to only then discover you don't have the capabilities or enough resources within your team to deliver on the improvement.

Five primary components for improvements exploration.

A great tool to consider is The Bute Group's new task template, this template looks at five components of new tasks:

Goals – What, why and when

It is vitally important to understand what your goal is. Within IT you may consider your goal for rolling out new software is to source and gain software approval. However, the real goal would be to have this rolled out across all applicable users.

Your goal would be the final step in the process, whilst one of your objectives would be to source software, and another would be to gain budget approval for the software. Have clarity around the 'what'. Know your 'why', why are you introducing this improvement? This should come easily from the earlier exercise.

You will recall, there are multiple parts to the why: yours, the business's, the team's and the individuals'; have clarity around why you would carry out the improvement for each of these areas.

Last and certainly not least, know when you aim to meet your goal, with milestones set for each objective, of course; it goes without writing, you do not need to be the one who carries this out. You have a pool of resources, gain their buy-in to the change and improvements, show your trust in them, delegate the tasks and authorisation and support them and the process.

Roles – What and who

When you consider roles, be role-specific and do not start with the available resources. If you focus on the roles that are required as opposed to the roles you have, you will get a clearer indication of your exact resources required to carry out the new improvements in full and successfully. If you only consider the current resource base, you are potentially trying to fit a square peg into a round hole.

Considering the required roles, expand your thinking outside of your immediately available resources and consider external resources that may be a support and have availability, e.g. finance, marketing, IT and HR etc.

Once you identify the roles required, at this point you can start to assign individuals to them. Remember, individuals like to be challenged and developed, and you may wish to entrust your team members to step up to a more challenging role as required in the initiative. You may also look to your colleagues within this senior management team to utilise some of their resources. With their permission, of course.

Processes – How

Processes are quite simply how the business improvement initiative is going to be carried out. This is potentially the most time-consuming of the five components; you will find that you would dip in and out of processes all the way through this as you introduce new elements and explore the required procedure updates. You may find this will be the last component you will complete on your task or project plan.

Environmental influences – What, where, when and who

Environmental influences are not relating to green environment thinking; however, you must, of course, with any business improvement or new initiative, take into account the impact of this on the environment. On this occasion, environmental influences refer to the influences outside of your direct control that will have an impact on the success or the limitations of your initiative.

Environmental influences take into account the barriers that may be put in place with areas such as the team working from geographically dispersed locations. The availability of external resources. The reduced budgets. Or alternatively, those forces that are working for you, although again, you have no direct control over, and that may be the availability of equipment and plant, the external support and so forth.

Communication – What, where, when why, who and how

Communication: you can put all the effort, time and energy into something, and without communicating it, no one will ever know. Understanding what is being communicated and to whom is your first step. Know your audience. Communicating a business improvement to the finance team will primarily be around numbers which would be different from your communication with IT, which will be around technology. Know your audience. What does your audience want to hear? This is not what you want to tell them. What you want to tell them, the message will be all about you whilst what they want to hear, the message will be tailored for them. Know your audience and their areas of interest.

Consider within your communication what platform are you going to communicate through, is it best to do this on video conference, email, face-to-face or phone? How about social media, LinkedIn or Instagram? Consider the platform that you want to be delivering your message on, which one will be most effective?

When is the best time to communicate, is it before, during or after the business improvement? Who do you need buy-in from? That will be anyone who could stop or make the business improvement difficult for you. That will be the individuals who are funding the initiative, the managers whose resources you will need to lean on, your manager, your team who will be delivering on this, you and the amount of time necessary to get this off the ground. This all needs to be communicated, and prior to communication, it needs to be thought through, articulated and then executed.

CHAPTER REFLECTION AND ACTION PLAN

Business initiatives focus in on improvements. This must be a responsibility you own and visit frequently.

CAMERON

As Cameron spends more time with her team and that of the senior management team, she could see that there was room for improvement. She had in the past been put off instigating anything other than the necessary improvements due to lack of resources. Now, she had clarity around what resources were required and the return on investment. She decided now was the time to work in more detail with the incident database. Along with her direct reports, they took a two-prong approach to business improvements. One was to address the top three items in the incident database, and the second was to look at longer term initiatives.

OVER TO YOU...

1. Ensure that your managers have been keeping the incident database up to date.

2. Arrange frequent meetings (if not already in place) to discuss solutions to the top recurring issues.

3. Consider the results from your Porter's five forces and the STEEPLE exercises, what initiatives could be introduced to start driving the business forward?

4. List these, including the cost, user, values and benefits, and all additional components.

CHAPTER 10

CHANGE MANAGEMENT

What a great place to start by having an initiative that will improve the business. The next part of the puzzle is how you implement the change. Managing change from the simplest through to complex changes can be time-consuming.

70% of change initiatives fail

When considering change it is not a one and done approach. Gallup research reports that 70% of change initiatives fail. 70%! That is a staggering number.

IMPROVEMENTS, IMPROVEMENTS AND IMPROVEMENTS

From your earlier exercise within continuous business improvements, you will have an understanding of why you are implementing the business improvement. I would like to take time to reiterate, change should only happen if there is an improvement. If you can't define the improvements, there is no reason for change. That doesn't mean that reactive change isn't an improvement; if you are making a change that stabilises a platform, a small process change that improves the user experience, or is quicker than before, that is an improvement and therefore requires change.

GET THE RIGHT PEOPLE AND LEVELS ON BOARD

This is worth repeating… Get the right people and levels on board from the start. You will require individuals who are on board with your proposal, who have influence within the business, who can authorise or have the ear of those who can authorise the change, those who have staying power. This is so important and therefore worth stating again, get the right people and levels on board from the start.

Consider who will be impacted by the change, be sure to go outside of the obvious. Who are the stakeholders, the individuals who have a vested interest in the change, and those who may not be in favour of the change? Who are the sponsors, those individuals who have asked for the change? They are often individuals within a senior role and are generally biased towards the success of the change. Who are the end-users, who is this directly going to impact? The end-user will be the individuals who will be working with the finished product or service.

Have you considered finance for budget sign off, marketing or sales, will your training department be expected to deliver the training on the end product or service? Who else needs to be included? Just a wee reminder, that to sell the change successfully to your audience, understand where their interest lies.

BRING PEOPLE ALONG WITH YOU

Humans like to be involved, we like to be seen to be important and have something to share, and that share is worth listening to. Take the pressure off yourself and consider a collaboration. Are there other senior managers who would collaborate with you on the change? Who would be an ambassador for the change? Consider people who have a lot to gain from the change; those would be ideal collaborators as they have a lot invested in the success.

If collaboration is not an option, at the very least, consider having a project team.

The project team should include representation from all the other departments that are impacted. Those individuals should be ambassadors for success. However, I have observed in the past where the project team has naysayers on the project, that these individuals feel personally responsible for highlighting everything and anything that will go wrong, without offering any solutions. Of course, part of the project team is to highlight and negate risks; however, the project team should be pulling in the same direction and looking for innovative solutions and successful execution.

Keep people in the loop and actively updated, be honest and open with your communication. If things are not going as planned, share the issues; however, be sure to have a plan for the resolution. It is uncomfortable for sponsors who have invested time, effort and potentially budgets in a change to hear things are going wrong and the change manager (who is often referred to as the project manager or change agent) has not thought through a solution for the issue.

ONE AND DONE

Introducing the change doesn't stop at the implementation. One of the many reasons that change implementation fails is when the implementation is seen as the final stage.

The change process often, if not always, requires a behavioural and mindset shift change for the users and potentially the business as a whole. Humans will take the path of least resistance and will revert to type, that is, working within their comfortable and habitual mindset and behaviour pattern. For change to be successful, consideration and review must continue after the implementation to ensure that the desired behaviours and mindsets are being demonstrated. After a period of time, this will become the users' new comfort zone.

Plan, implement change, review, action plan, implement, review, action plan, implement... when and only when both the change has completed a couple of clean review rounds without updating the action plan, and the resources are delivering the process without error, should it be signed off. Do not be tempted to sign the change off too early, 70% of changes fail. Get it right, ensure the changes are sustainable, gather sign off and execute the final handover plans.

KEEP YOUR FOCUS

Complex changes are not quick. Simple changes are. However, they deserve the same attention to detail and process as the more complex changes. Plan, implement, review and repeat.

RESULTS DRIVEN

Mentioned earlier in the book is the results-driven mindset, this should be the norm for a senior manager. And this must be part of the mindset for change management. Change results in improvements, but how do you measure those improvements? Monetary value? Increased outputs? Faster end-user use? Bigger? Smaller? Customer satisfaction results will be fundamental to your measurement of success and what you as the manager will be measured on, both formal measurements and personal reputation and brand. Ensure that you understand and communicate to everyone involved what you and the business are measuring the success on.

When others hear of your initiatives, they will all want a say and a piece of the action... what bells and whistles can they have? Assertive thinking is required here; be wise on what you propose the KPIs are, be selective on what additional points you agree to. Keep in mind this has an impact on resources usage and budget. Do not set yourself or your teams up for failure.

Change plans often look like a project plan; there will be a goal with an associated date. The goal should be chunked down into manageable steps or objectives that, although challenging and exciting, feels doable. These steps, often referred to as milestones, will be accompanied by details and be assigned a deadline date. There is often a lot more detail around each milestone. Depending on the complexity, it will often include a breakdown on the steps within the milestone, that may include communication plans, budget forecast vs actual, KPIs, meetings to update sponsors and stakeholders on progress. If the milestone is perceived as being simple, then the detail is often simple.

There should be an alignment between complexity and the simplicity of the change, and this should be reflected on the level of detail to include within the milestones. Keep it as simple as possible. Even when working with complex changes, there is a requirement to present plans that your audience can understand.

MOST PEOPLE HAVE A DAY JOB

Consider that most people working on the change initiative will likely have their day job. This has been a bone of contention for a lot of change and project managers; they don't believe or are simply not getting access to the resource for the agreed or required time. Or that they themselves, the change manager, are unable to allocate the required time to manage the change implementation effectively. This will play a big part in the statistic of 70% of change initiatives fail. Ensure you have the time and resources to dedicate to the initiative, and any external resources are agreed upfront before you commit to the change. Dependencies and assumptions must be noted, and risk assessed. Do not set yourself up for failure.

TEAM DEVELOPMENT

When bringing together a project team or creating a new team from scratch, there are several stages that will naturally occur during the development and maturity of the team. Forming, storming, norming and performing is a concept by Bruce Tuckman in 1965.

When introducing a change that impacts your teams directly, it is important to recognise the phases that the team is currently operating within. Depending upon the complexity of the change, and how this is perceived by the team, or end user, there is likely to be a backward step in the team development phase.

Recognising which team phase your team currently sits within will be important, not least from a timing and deadline perspective, also for future planning.

Forming

The forming stage is the first phase of team development. That is when the team is coming together, whether that be for a new long-term role or department or a short-term project. The forming stage typically demonstrates individuals' level of apprehension, unsure of themselves, and quiet. Whilst they may understand the role, i.e. finance manager, ICT manager, senior manager, there will be a level of uncertainty around the responsibilities. You as a senior manager, will play a large part in how long this takes; the more unsure individuals are, the quieter and less confident, the longer it will take to move into storming phase.

The energy at this point may be flat, and you will be wanting to have the team talking and interacting together.

Storming

Once the team feel more comfortable with each other, they will start to test the boundaries. Part of this stage is the individual displaying their aspirations and asserting themselves within the team; they will start to vie for position, not their job role, more of how they will fit into the bigger picture within the team. As a senior manager, you will want to observe how people are behaving and their attitudes and mindsets during this phase. You will observe people's career aspirations, those who want to become managers and team leaders, those who want to come in, do the job and go home, those who want to be seen as experts etc. Some individuals will want to take on more work, while others will push back on the work being asked of them. This is a very much needed phase and should not be hurried. It's a sign of an immature manager when they push the team through this stage too quickly.

There will be high energy levels in this phase; some people may feel very uncomfortable with the storming stage while others will be relishing it.

Within this phase, you will be wanting to observe and respond to the team's behaviours, recognising good behaviour, quashing inappropriate behaviour, and reinforcing boundaries.

Norming

The norming stage is where people have found their place within the team; they will be socialising together and possibly breaking into their own clique. Typically, the team will be working towards the goal. It will feel more relaxed than the storming stage.

The energy will be typically less than the storming stage. You will start to observe the 'influencers' within the team. These will be the individuals who others are likely to listen to and follow; they are not always in a senior role. These individuals are worth taking note of, and they may change over time.

Performing

The performing stage leads to the magic. There is typically a higher energy, and the team are working as one and towards a common goal. At this stage, the team will be more independent, less needy of your time. With energy levels higher, you will be ideally delegating more and harnessing the productivity to stretch the existing goals. Motivation is high, and this is reflected in the level of productivity.

As the senior manager, understanding the team development phases is important to offer effective support to your team through the change. Acknowledging and preparing for the shift in the development phase if a change is perceived as complex is necessary. The shift will often result in a dip in productivity, understanding what this may mean in terms of numbers (remember results-driven), and to manage the expectations of others during this period is crucial. It will allow you to plan for and readdress the productivity loss when the team is back to the performing stage.

Understanding the requirements of your initiative, the consideration on your team, and importantly the impact it has on the individuals will give you the tools to support the team through the changes the initiatives brings.

THE CHANGE CURVE

When a complex change is introduced to the team, some or all of the team will be impacted by this. This is not a one size fits all impact. You or others may consider a change implementation as simple, and other members will find it complex and vice versa. The change curve will support you in knowing where your team members are in terms of performance and motivation. It is very unlikely that your team will be at the same stage all the way through, if at all. There are eight stages.

1. Unsubstantiated bias

Unsubstantiated bias is stage one of the process. This is where office gossip kicks in. This almost exclusively happens when the changes are large and complex, reorganisation, large roll-out of new automation software, merging of companies, new management, etc. The gossip is generally based on hearsay and leans primarily on the negative. Your role is to clarify the facts.

2. Disbelief

The disbelief stage can be based on what was heard at stage one, and how the facts that you present are different from what was expected.

Depending on the complexity of the perceived change, at this stage where those impacted (and often those not directly impacted) find the change too difficult to comprehend, there can be thoughts and gossip on 'why change something that works' or 'I can't believe this is what is happening, they are clearly setting us up for redundancy' and such like.

As a senior manager, it is hoped you will have taken the time and made a real effort to build a meaningful relationship with your teams, through 1:1s and skip level 1:1s. This will have gone some way to creating a solid level of trust and shared goals and values. It is important at this stage (and all stages) that you do not become known as a gossiper, do not partake in the ritual, being known as a gossip will ring the death toll on your personal reputation and brand, no one will trust you, not even those who you gossip with.

If, however, you are one of the 81% that your employees would not hire back as their manager, then the 'disbelief' stage will take longer to move on from. You as a senior manager must address the gossip with facts and confidence.

3. Resentment

The teams should now have the facts from you (or possibly their direct manager, your direct report). At the resentment stage, individuals are talking amongst themselves around the negatives of the proposed change, this is not being shared with you as their manager. There are lots of private conversations on what the negative impact will be, how it will look, what it will mean. These are often passive-aggressive conversations, throwaway comments from the team during team meetings, within 1:1s, it is not a direct comment, it is often delivered in a passive manner.

4. Open anger

The open anger stage is when the manager can expect to be confronted and hear all the grievances. Open anger is not physical, and that should certainly not be tolerated, nor should verbal abuse. Your individual team members may be demonstrating this with exasperation and a raised volume, not shouting or screaming. You must allow the individuals to speak, the content of the conversation can be very personal to an individual, and they need the time to be heard. The individual often masks the conversation by using terms such as 'we' instead of 'I', and 'us' instead of 'me'. It is important to understand the individual's points. The team members will have different points and be travelling along the curve at different speeds.

This stage is a good stage; it allows the individual to vent, then they will be in a better position to listen to you and will start to be more open to moving forward.

5. Negotiation

The open anger stage has passed, you will see productivity very slowly improving, although it will still be lower than prior to the change. At the negotiation stage, the individual is now working (albeit, slowly) with the change; however, they will want to test boundaries, and there is a need for them to try to make something happen that will work for them. Negotiation begins; it can often be those impacted who will want to negotiate on how to get things back to 'normal'.

For you, this stage is another opportunity to reinforce boundaries. However, negotiate and compromise, and where possible, be open to the individual's input. Do not compromise the validity of the change initiative.

6. Trial and error

Productivity is on the incline, and the trial and error stage is where the changes are being implemented. Depending on the mindset of the individual, there may be lots of errors, proving the change decision was the wrong one and they the users were right, and had you listened to them at the negotiation stage, these errors would not have happened. This is typical human behaviour; we want to be right. There will be a learning curve for those who want to genuinely 'see what happens', even those individuals may come back with genuine errors.

Trial and error is an opportunity to refine your change implementation as part of the plan, implement change, review, action plan, implement, review, action plan, implement cycle. Do not dismiss the errors being highlighted, it is better to capture them in trial stage and resolve before going live.

7. Conscious acceptance

Now there is a real shift of mindset and behaviour; productivity is at an all-time high. Particularly as the change implementation was a definite improvement. People are realising and accepting that the change is happening and working and was worth the perceived pain. They start to accept the changes, some begrudgingly, others openly. There is a shift in productivity; teams are moving from 'Norming' to 'Performing' stage.

8. BAU delivery

This stage is unconscious acceptance. The new change is no longer thought about and is accepted as the norm. Delivery should be as expected, and this should be at a greater rate than pre-change. After all, any change implementation should be both results-driven and an improvement.

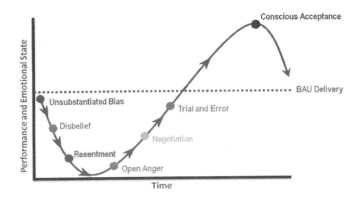

Adapted from The Bute Group (2019)

BACK UP AND ROLLBACK

Should the worst case scenario happen, and the change initiative is not going according to plan, always have a back-up plan, typically referred to as a rollback plan. The rollback plan should be a thought through and a mature plan that can be implemented at a moment's notice. As you consider the rollback plan, consider the implications of the rollback impact on the business, costs, productivity, business reputation and brand. Consider the implications to the team, for the additional resources that have been assigned to the change implementation and, of course, for you.

It is better to have and execute a rollback plan and be able to fix the issues before complete disaster than do nothing and cross your fingers and hope for the best. I have worked in places where scenarios have been set up and executed and the measurement of success was based on the rollback plan. It is better to be prepared than be caught without a solution to a potential problem. Within reason of course.

Consider who and what has to be on standby for the rollback. Be prepared.

CHAPTER REFLECTION AND ACTION PLAN

Change is necessary for a company to remain in business. Change initiatives should only be implemented when the improvements outweigh the cost and the temporary impact of lower motivation and productivity.

CAMERON

Cameron had several initiatives she wanted to implement, several from the incident database and several proactive initiatives. She stepped back to consider the bigger picture. Within IT, if they resolved the top three incidents, this would release 35% of the working week across the team. There would be concern about what this would mean to headcount. However, if she piggybacked a proactive initiative, she could transfer the freed-up time to proactive and enhanced offerings.

Within the weekly discussions, it was clear that IT was hesitant to proceed for fear of job losses. However, Cameron very openly and honestly discussed what the alternatives were, including the small chance of redundancy. It became clear this had an impact on the

IT team who went from norming back to storming; the team were vying to make themselves more needed to the business. Cameron could see she had her work cut out. She needed to tread softly and assuredly. As she has for all the chapters, Cameron completed the exercises.

OVER TO YOU...

1. Observe your teams, and with your direct reports' input, gauge which team development phase your team currently sits within.

2. List your initiatives under two columns: proactive and reactive.

3. Is your team in a healthy team development phase to take on a new initiative and change?

4. What impact will the change have on your team?

5. Who else outside of your team must be engaged?

6. How complex is the change?

7. Do you have the experience and want to manage the project?

8. Are there quick wins that can be implemented for your team?

There are so many questions and levels of change that I would recommend that, if need be, you collaborate with someone who knows the business better and is a good project manager. This is a great learning opportunity for you. Don't waste it; don't allow your ego to get in the way of asking for support and guidance.

DEMONSTRATE YOUR WORTH TO YOUR MANAGER AND THE BUSINESS

It is time to step out of your own shadow and show your worth to your manager, peers and the business. New managers can lack credibility, particularly when starting a new role within a new company. It is important that you network and market yourself without aggression and arrogance. It's important that others know the capabilities and the value you bring to the role.

Self-marketing is an art; it is not about being all about you. Arrogance is easy to spot – it is all about you, what you've done, what you achieved, what you're working on, what recognition you received and so forth and bears no relevance to the receiving party. Ego is an interesting subject; ego is your social mask. Your social mask is what you would like to portray to others; it can be a driver and a push for standards, do not see it as a negative aspect, just ensure that you manage it and use it wisely.

People are fearful of letting others know what they have done, then get annoyed when no recognition is given. It is not your manager or colleagues' job to have to go looking for what you've been working on. Keep a regular channel open to update your manager and others on your progress and changes. Consider ways that you would be comfortable sharing the news, be clear on when to use the words 'I' or 'we'. 'We' is to be used when you are part of a bigger group, which is potentially something you've achieved with your team. 'I' is to be used when you have achieved something.

KNOW YOUR WORTH

Do not let imposter syndrome get in the way. Keep a record of what you are working on. It is great to refer back to when you are feeling low, or have a progress update meeting with your manager. The record does not need to be detailed, just enough to remind you of what you have been doing and what you are looking to work on.

Look at the roles and responsibilities, be prepared to share when you have exceeded the expectations. Those expectations are based on your job role and responsibilities. What would be of interest to the receiving party? Consider as you share your achievements with others, have you asked them about their achievements? Are you giving others the opportunity to share their successes with you?

LAW OF BALANCE

By sharing the good times, it requires (law of balance) that you take responsibility for the areas that did not or are not going so well. It can't be one way; it must be a balanced approach. Equally, do not focus solely on what did not work, take a balanced approach to this.

Repeat for the final time in this book, "I am worth the investment."

You have got this, and it only leaves me to say I wish you the very best of luck.

REFERENCES

Ariely, D. (2009) *Predictably Irrational: The Hidden Forces that Shape Our Decisions* [ebook reader], HarperCollins.

Briskin, A. (1998) *The stirring of soul in the workplace.* 1st ed. San Francisco: Berrett-Koehler Publishers.

Clifton, J. (2017) *The World's Broken Workplace* [Online]. Available at https://news.gallup.com/opinion/chairman/212045/world-broken-workplace.aspx (Accessed 24 October 2020).

Colmean, D. (2009) *Emotional Intelligence: Why It Can Matter More Than IQ* [ebook reader], Bloomsbury Publishing.

Gallup, (2017) *State of the Global Workplace* [Online]. Available at https://www.gallup.com/workplace/238079/state-global-workplace-2017.aspx#formheader (Accessed 27 September 2020).

Gardner, H. (2008) *Multiple Intelligences: New Horizons in Theory and Practice* [ebook reader], Basic Books.

Harvard Business Review (1996) *What Is Strategy?* [Online]. Available at https://hbr.org/1996/11/what-is-strategy (Accessed 24 September 2020).

Johnson, G., Scholes, K, and Whittington, R. (2005) *Exploring Corporate Strategy*, London: Prentice Hall.

Leonard, D. and Coltea, C. (2013) *Most Change Initiatives Fail -- But They Don't Have To* [Online]. Available at https://news.gallup.com/businessjournal/162707/change-initiatives-fail-don.aspx (Accessed 01 December 2020).

Schwartz, S. H. (1992) Universals in the content and structure of values: theoretical advances and empirical tests in 20 countries. In M. P. Zonna (Ed.), Advances in experimental social psychology (pp. 1–66). San Diego, CA: Academic Press.

The Bute Group (2021) *Out with the old, in with the new,* London: The Bute Group

The Bute Group (2019) *Foundations of Change*, London: The Bute Group.

ABOUT THE AUTHOR

Margo Manning has worked in the development arena for over 30 years. In the last 20 years, she has been delivering as one of the UK's top Leadership and Management Coaches and Facilitators.

Margo's first book, *The Step-Up Mindset for New Managers,* was a No. 1 Amazon bestseller.

Margo travels the globe working with international companies that are looking to develop their managers and leaders. She works with top FTSE 100 companies and more.

NOTES